HEINEMANN MATHEMATICS 2

Name

WORKBOOK 4

Addition and Subtraction to 13, Halves and Quarters

Revised

Islands

Use cubes to add.

Use pennies. How much is it to go to

Mango Island and Nim-Nam-Noo ☐ p

Nim-Nam-Noo and Bear Island ☐ p ?

Use cubes to subtract. Match each boat to an island.

Write a subtraction story on this boat.

Extension

Amy and Jack go to Mango Island.
How much has each left?

Amy ____ p

Jack ____ p

To land on the island, find numbers which add to 11.

Use counters.

10 + 1				

How many ? ___
3 fly away.

11 − 3 = ___

How many ? ___
7 fall off.

11 − 7 = ___

How many ? ___
5 are picked.

11 − 5 = ___

How many ? ___
9 hide.

11 − 9 = ___

Bushes

Each bush has 11 flowers. Write stories.

9 + 2 = 11

2 + 9 = 11

11 − 2 = 9

11 − 9 = 2

8 + 3 =

3 + 8 =

11 − 3 =

11 − 8 =

7 + 4 =

4 + 7 =

11 − 4 =

11 − 7 =

6 + 5 =

5 + 6 =

11 − 5 =

11 − 6 =

Investigation

Find sets of 3 numbers which add to 11.

In the jungle

$$\begin{array}{r} 4 \\ +7 \\ \hline \\ \hline \end{array} \qquad \begin{array}{r} 11 \\ -3 \\ \hline \\ \hline \end{array} \qquad \begin{array}{r} 3 \\ +8 \\ \hline \\ \hline \end{array} \qquad \begin{array}{r} 11 \\ -9 \\ \hline \\ \hline \end{array} \qquad \begin{array}{r} 11 \\ -6 \\ \hline \\ \hline \end{array}$$

11 − 4 = ___

11 − 8 = ___

5 + 6 = ___

11 − 2 = ___

11 − 1 = ___

The nest has 11 eggs.
4 fall out.

How many left? ___

11 flies
5 ants
How many more flies? ___

3 + 4 + 4 = ___

5 + 2 + 3 = ___

Buying food

How much does each spend?

Each child has 11p. They buy these things.
How much has each left?

Problem solving

Spend 11p.
What 3 things will you buy?

Nim-Nam-Noo

Put 12 Nim-nams on the island like this.

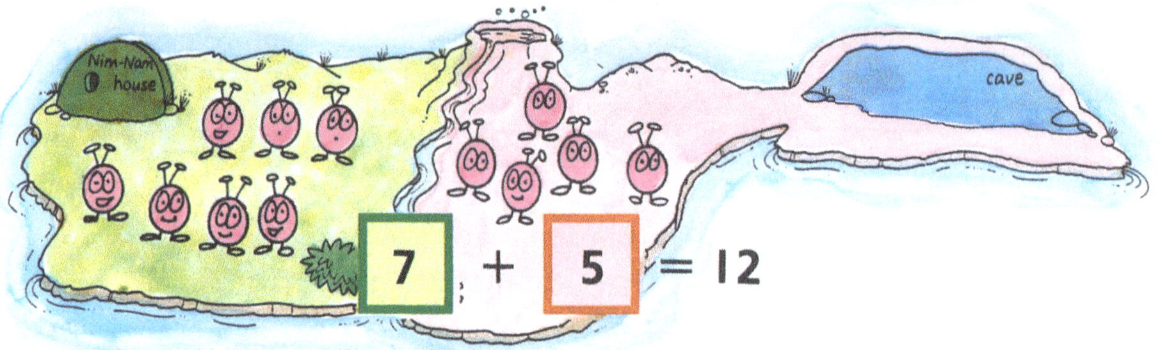

Find other ways to put 12 Nim-nams on the island.

☐ + ☐ = 12   ☐ + ☐ = 12

☐ + ☐ = 12   ☐ + ☐ = 12

☐ + ☐ = 12   ☐ + ☐ = 12

☐ + ☐ = 12   ☐ + ☐ = 12

Put 12 Nim-nams on the island like this.

5 + 4 + 3 = 12

Find other ways.

☐ + ☐ + ☐ = 12

☐ + ☐ + ☐ = 12

☐ + ☐ + ☐ = 12

Put 12 Nim-nams on the island.

If Noo eats 5, how many are left?

12 – 5 = ☐

12 – 9 = ☐ 12 – 4 = ☐ 12 – 10 = ☐

12 – 7 = ☐ 12 – 6 = ☐ 12 – 3 = ☐

Nim-nams

7 + 5 =

12 – 5 =

12 – 7 =

5 + 7 =

9 + 3 =

3 + 9 =

12 – 3 =

12 – 9 =

6 + 6 =

12 – 6 =

8 + 4 =

4 + 8 =

12 – 4 =

12 – 8 =

Nim-nam house

Find the answers. Colour them.

red	7 + 3	12 − 10	12 − 7
blue	12 − 4	8 + 3	6 + 6
green	6 + 3	12 − 9	12 − 8

How many altogether?

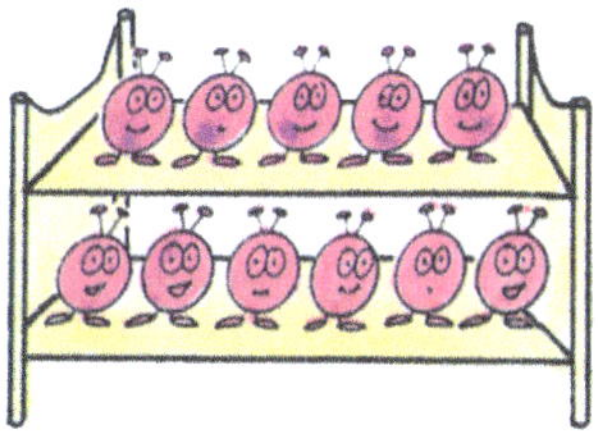

$\begin{array}{r} 5 \\ +6 \\ \hline \end{array}$ $\begin{array}{r} 8 \\ +4 \\ \hline \end{array}$ $\begin{array}{r} 7 \\ +5 \\ \hline \end{array}$ $\begin{array}{r} 3 \\ +9 \\ \hline \end{array}$

$\begin{array}{r} 5 \\ +7 \\ \hline \end{array}$ $\begin{array}{r} 6 \\ +6 \\ \hline \end{array}$ $\begin{array}{r} 3 \\ 4 \\ +5 \\ \hline \end{array}$ $\begin{array}{r} 6 \\ 4 \\ +2 \\ \hline \end{array}$ $\begin{array}{r} 4 \\ 4 \\ +3 \\ \hline \end{array}$

Bear Island

In each cave, colour three bears that add to make 12.

The school cave has

an even answer greater than 10.

Write **School** above the school cave.

Extension

Use these numbers to make the sums.

9 8 4 3

8 + 4 = 12	+ ___ = 11	+ ___ = 12	+ ___ = 13
− ___ = 4	− ___ = 6	− ___ = 1	− ___ = 5

Fun Island

Use 13 counters.

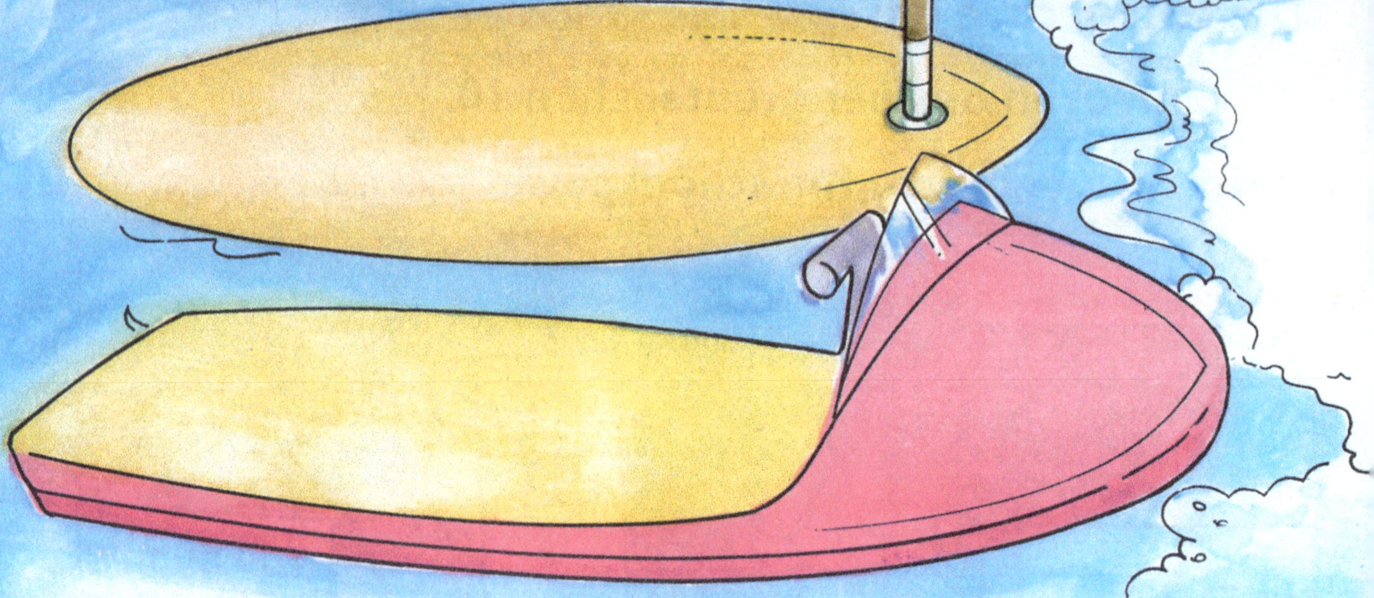

$$\begin{array}{r} 6 \\ +7 \\ \hline \\ \hline \end{array}$$

$$\begin{array}{r} + \\ \hline \\ \hline \end{array}$$

Find other stories for 13.

$\begin{array}{r} + \\ \hline 13 \\ \hline \end{array}$	$\begin{array}{r} + \\ \hline 13 \\ \hline \end{array}$	$\begin{array}{r} + \\ \hline 13 \\ \hline \end{array}$	$\begin{array}{r} + \\ \hline 13 \\ \hline \end{array}$	$\begin{array}{r} + \\ \hline 13 \\ \hline \end{array}$	$\begin{array}{r} + \\ \hline 13 \\ \hline \end{array}$

$2 + 3 + 8 = 13$

Find more stories like this for 13.

6 + 7 = 13

7 + 6 =

13 − 6 =

13 − 7 =

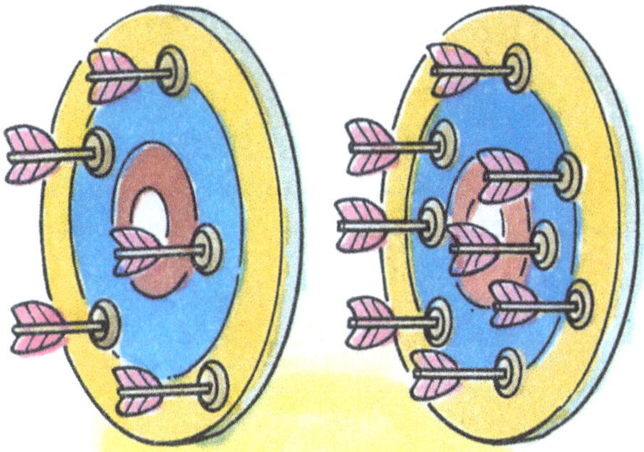

5 + 8 =

8 + 5 =

13 − 5 =

13 − 8 =

9 + 4 =

4 + 9 =

13 − 9 =

13 − 4 =

10 + 3 =

3 + 10 =

13 − 10 =

13 − 3 =

R24

Train ride

Colour a carriage to match each answer.

Subtract 5 from 13

Subtract 3 from 12

6 less than 13

3 less than 13

4 more than 9

2 more than 10

Spooky Castle

Write the missing number.

This key opens the door.

Cross out flies to make 13.

13 children go in.
8 come out.

How many are still in? ____

Add to find the one that is different.

The trapdoor key is in it.

Escape

Write the answers.

$7 + 6 =$

$4 + 8 =$

$12 - 3 =$

$13 - 4 =$

$11 - 9 =$

$7 + 4 =$

$11 - 4 =$

$12 - 6 =$

$13 - 6 =$

Colour the boxes

blue if the answer is odd,

red if the answer is even.

5	12	9	8	7	13
+8	−9	+4	+5	+5	−8

Which door has an even answer? Colour it red.

Problem solving

Amy had 13p.
She lost 7p in the sea.

How much is left? ___ p

Colour the monster that has two more black spots than green spots.

Find chests with the same answer.
Colour them to match.

The treasure is in the white chest.
Mark it ✗.

Stickers

Problem solving / Extension

Find the cost of a fox and a bear. ____

Find the cost of a fox, a tiger and a dog. ____

I spend 13p.
I buy 2 animals.
What do I buy? ____________

I have 8p.
I want a panda.
How much more do I need? ____

I have 12p. I buy a bear.
What else can I now buy?

fox or ________ or ________

Prizes

Now do these.

7 + 9 = ☐   6 + 8 = ☐   10 + 9 = ☐

16 − 7 = ☐   14 − 8 = ☐   17 − 9 = ☐

Who wins a prize? (✓)

4 + 8 + 3 + 4 = ____

9 + 2 + 5 + 2 = ____

8 + 6 + 7 − 2 = ____

Halves

You need

Fold each in half.

Colour one half of each shape.

Tick the shapes that show halves.

Making halves

Cut out the four-strip.

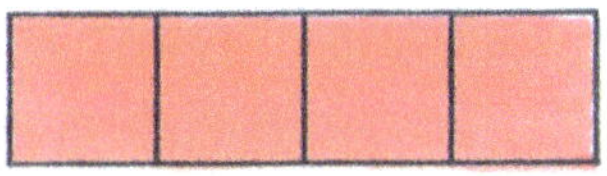

Fold it in half.

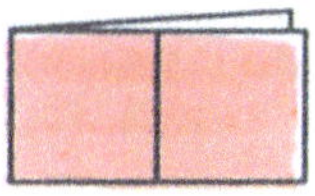

One half of 4 is ___ .

Cut out the six-strip.

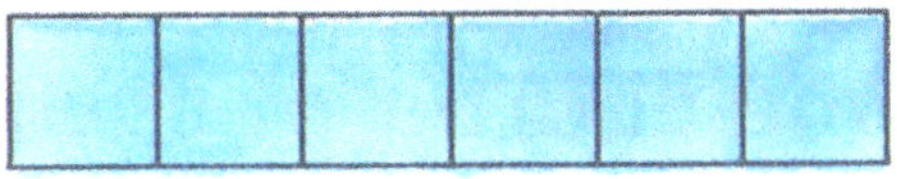

Fold it in half.

One half of 6 is ___ .

Make a tower with 8 cubes.

Halve it like this →

One half of 8 is ___ .

Use 10 cubes.

One half of 10 is ___ .

Use cubes. One half of 12 is ___ .

One half of 16 is ___ .

One half of 20 is ___ .

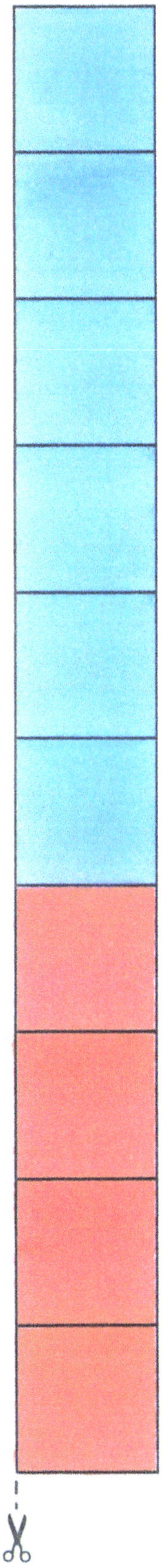

Quarters

You need

Fold each in quarters.

Colour one quarter of each shape.

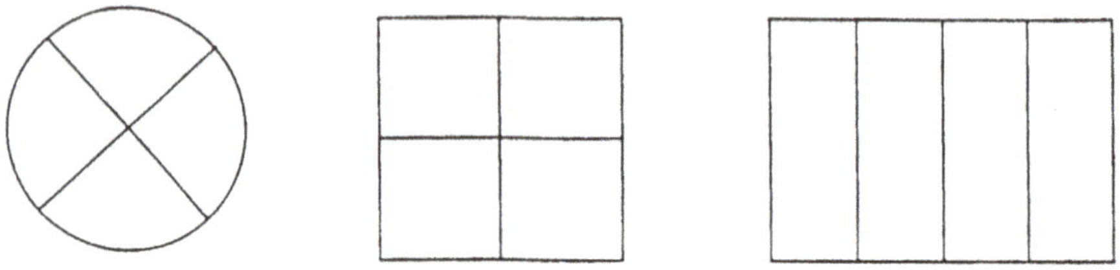

Tick the shapes that show quarters.

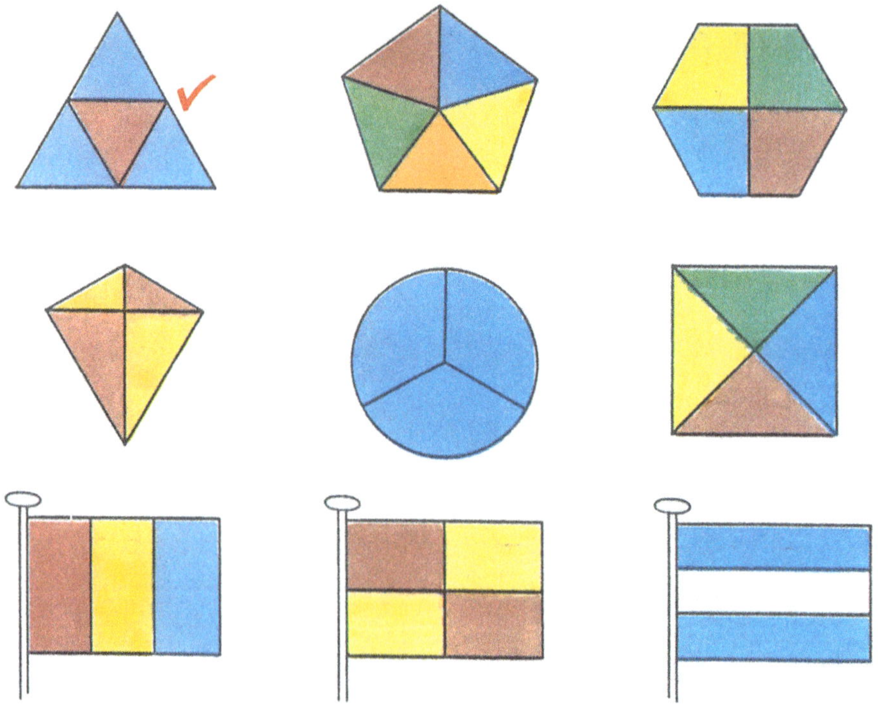

1	2	3	4	5	6	7	8	9	10	11	12	13	14	15	16	17	18	19	20	21	22	23

Heinemann is an imprint of Pearson Education Limited, a company incorporated in England and Wales, having its registered office at Edinburgh Gate, Harlow, Essex, CM20 2JE. Registered company number: 872828
ISBN 978 0 435 03094 0
First published 1991. Revised edition 1995. 19 28
Typeset and Illustrated by Oxprint Design. Printed and bound in Great Britain

ISBN 978-0-435030-94-0

SPMG

HEINEMANN MATHEMATICS 2

Name

WORKBOOK 4

Addition and Subtraction to 13, Halves and Quarters

Revised

Islands

Use cubes to add.

Use pennies. How much is it to go to

Mango Island and Nim-Nam-Noo ☐ p

Nim-Nam-Noo and Bear Island ☐ p ?

Use cubes to subtract. Match each boat to an island.

Write a subtraction story on this boat.

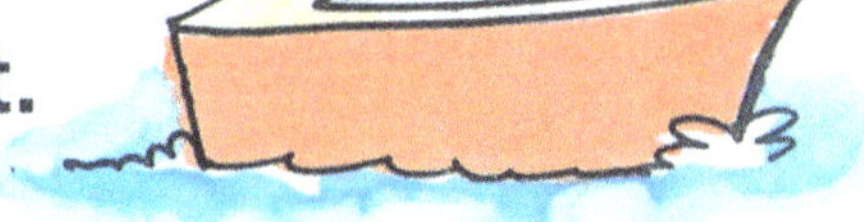

Extension

Amy and Jack go to Mango Island.
How much has each left?

Amy ___ p

Jack ___ p

To land on the island, find numbers which add to 11.

Use counters.

10 + 1				

How many  ? ____
3 fly away.

11 − 3 = ____

How many  ? ____
5 are picked.

11 − 5 = ____

How many  ? ____
7 fall off.

11 − 7 = ____

How many  ? ____
9 hide.

11 − 9 = ____

Bushes

Each bush has 11 flowers. Write stories.

9 + 2 = 11

2 + 9 = 11

11 – 2 = 9

11 – 9 = 2

8 + 3 =

3 + 8 =

11 – 3 =

11 – 8 =

7 + 4 =

4 + 7 =

11 – 4 =

11 – 7 =

6 + 5 =

5 + 6 =

11 – 5 =

11 – 6 =

Investigation

Find sets of 3 numbers which add to 11.

In the jungle

$$\begin{array}{r} 4 \\ +7 \\ \hline \\ \hline \end{array}$$

$$\begin{array}{r} 11 \\ -3 \\ \hline \\ \hline \end{array}$$

$$\begin{array}{r} 3 \\ +8 \\ \hline \\ \hline \end{array}$$

$$\begin{array}{r} 11 \\ -9 \\ \hline \\ \hline \end{array}$$

$$\begin{array}{r} 11 \\ -6 \\ \hline \\ \hline \end{array}$$

11 – 4 = ____

11 – 8 = ____

5 + 6 = ____

11 – 2 = ____

11 – 1 = ____

The nest has 11 eggs.
4 fall out.

How many left? ____

11 flies
5 ants
How many more flies? ____

3 + 4 + 4 = ____

5 + 2 + 3 = ____

Buying food

How much does each spend?

Each child has 11p. They buy these things.
How much has each left?

Problem solving

Spend 11p.
What 3 things will you buy?

Nim-Nam-Noo

Put 12 Nim-nams on the island like this.

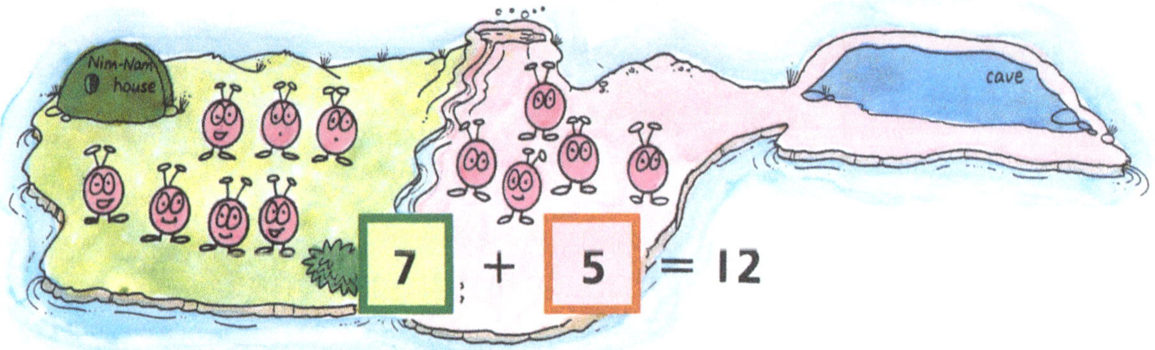

7 + 5 = 12

Find other ways to put 12 Nim-nams on the island.

□ + □ = 12   □ + □ = 12

□ + □ = 12   □ + □ = 12

□ + □ = 12   □ + □ = 12

□ + □ = 12   □ + □ = 12

Put 12 Nim-nams on the island like this.

$5 + 4 + 3 = 12$

Find other ways.

$\square + \square + \square = 12$

$\square + \square + \square = 12$

$\square + \square + \square = 12$

Put 12 Nim-nams on the island.

If Noo eats 5, how many are left?

$12 - 5 = \square$

$12 - 9 = \square$ $\quad 12 - 4 = \square$ $\quad 12 - 10 = \square$

$12 - 7 = \square$ $\quad 12 - 6 = \square$ $\quad 12 - 3 = \square$

Nim-nams

7 + 5 =

12 − 5 =

12 − 7 =

5 + 7 =

9 + 3 =

3 + 9 =

12 − 3 =

12 − 9 =

6 + 6 =

12 − 6 =

8 + 4 =

4 + 8 =

12 − 4 =

12 − 8 =

Nim-nam house

Find the answers. Colour them.

red	7 + 3	12 − 10	12 − 7
blue	12 − 4	8 + 3	6 + 6
green	6 + 3	12 − 9	12 − 8

How many altogether?

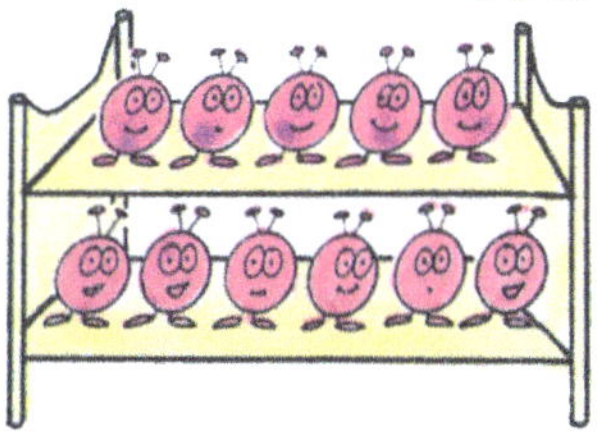

$$\begin{array}{r} 5 \\ +6 \\ \hline \\ \hline \end{array} \quad \begin{array}{r} 8 \\ +4 \\ \hline \\ \hline \end{array} \quad \begin{array}{r} 7 \\ +5 \\ \hline \\ \hline \end{array} \quad \begin{array}{r} 3 \\ +9 \\ \hline \\ \hline \end{array}$$

$$\begin{array}{r} 5 \\ +7 \\ \hline \\ \hline \end{array} \quad \begin{array}{r} 6 \\ +6 \\ \hline \\ \hline \end{array} \quad \begin{array}{r} 3 \\ 4 \\ +5 \\ \hline \\ \hline \end{array} \quad \begin{array}{r} 6 \\ 4 \\ +2 \\ \hline \\ \hline \end{array} \quad \begin{array}{r} 4 \\ 4 \\ +3 \\ \hline \\ \hline \end{array}$$

Bear Island

In each cave,
colour **three** bears that add to make 12.

The school cave has

an even answer greater than 10.

Write **School** above the school cave.

Use these numbers to make the sums.

9 8 4 3

8 + 4 = 12	+ = 11	+ = 12	+ = 13
− = 4	− = 6	− = 1	− = 5

Fun Island

Use 13 counters.

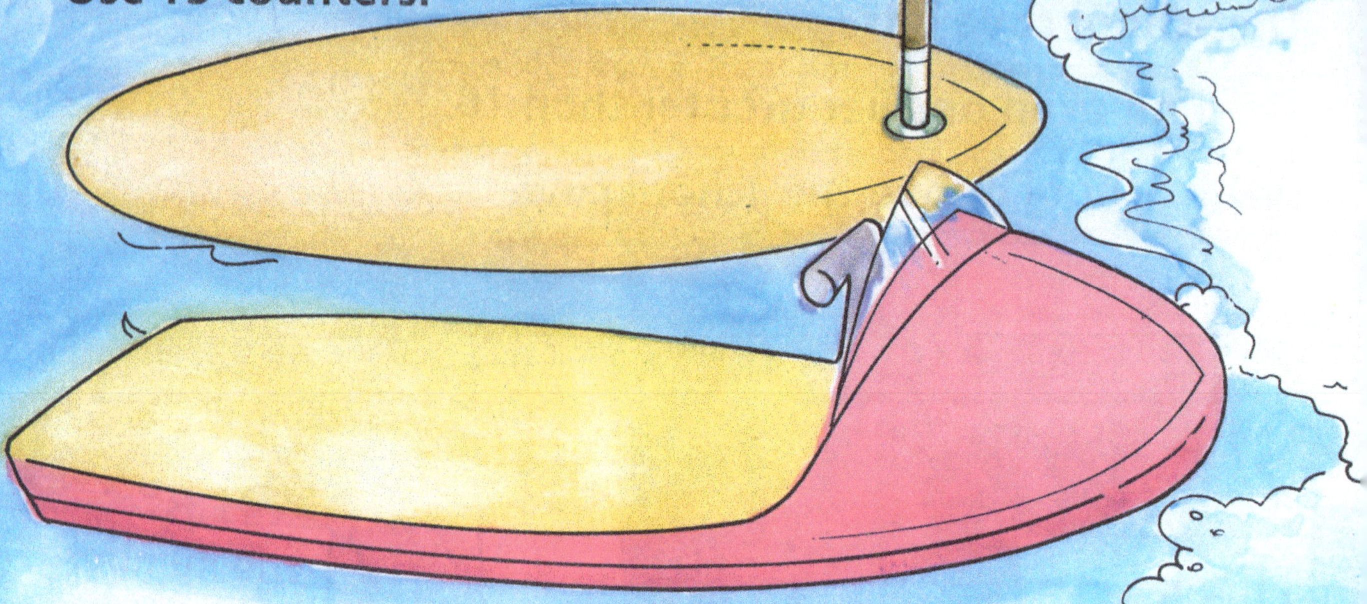

6
+7
___

___

+
___

___

Find other stories for 13.

+	+	+	+	+	+
13	13	13	13	13	13

$2 + 3 + 8 = 13$

Find more stories like this for 13.

6 + 7 = 13

7 + 6 =

13 − 6 =

13 − 7 =

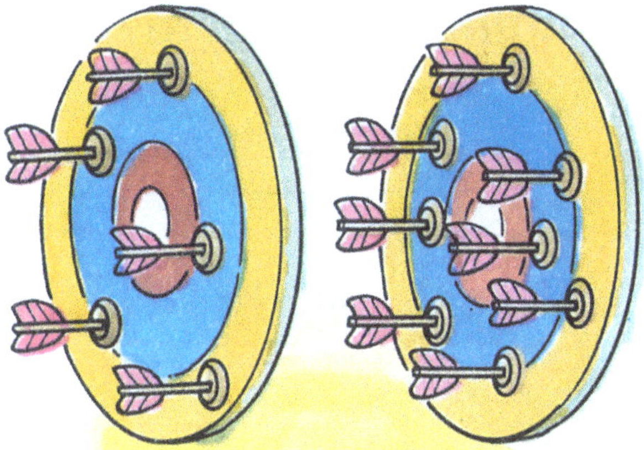

5 + 8 =

8 + 5 =

13 − 5 =

13 − 8 =

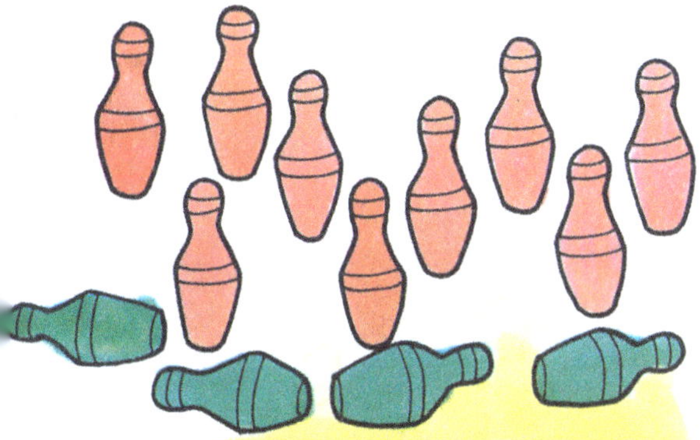

9 + 4 =

4 + 9 =

13 − 9 =

13 − 4 =

10 + 3 =

3 + 10 =

13 − 10 =

13 − 3 =

R24

Train ride

Colour a carriage to match each answer.

Spooky Castle

Write the missing number.

This key opens the door.

Cross out flies to make 13.

13 children go in.
8 come out.

How many are still in? ___

Add to find the one that is different. ✓

The trapdoor key is in it.

Escape

Write the answers.

$7 + 6 =$	
$4 + 8 =$	
$12 - 3 =$	
$13 - 4 =$	
$11 - 9 =$	
$7 + 4 =$	
$11 - 4 =$	
$12 - 6 =$	
$13 - 6 =$	

Colour the boxes

blue if the answer is odd,

red if the answer is even.

5	12	9	8	7	13
+8	−9	+4	+5	+5	−8
___	___	___	___	___	___

Which door has an even answer? Colour it red.

Problem solving

Colour three numbers which add to 12.

Amy had 13p.
She lost 7p in the sea.

How much is left? ___ p

Colour the monster that has two more black spots than green spots.

Find chests with the same answer.
Colour them to match.

The treasure is in the white chest.
Mark it ✗.

Stickers

Problem solving / Extension

Find the cost of a fox and a bear. ____

Find the cost of a fox, a tiger and a dog. ____

I spend 13p.
I buy 2 animals.
What do I buy? ____________

I have 8p.
I want a panda.
How much more do I need? ____

I have 12p. I buy a bear.
What else can I now buy?

fox or ________ or ________

Prizes

8. [+] [7] [=] ______

15. [−] [6] [=] ______

Now do these.

7 + 9 = ☐ 6 + 8 = ☐ 10 + 9 = ☐

16 − 7 = ☐ 14 − 8 = ☐ 17 − 9 = ☐

Who wins a prize? (✓)

[4] [+] [8] [+] [3] [+] [4] [=] ______

[9] [+] [2] [+] [5] [+] [2] [=] ______

[8] [+] [6] [+] [7] [−] [2] [=] ______

Halves

You need

Fold each in half.

Colour one half of each shape.

Tick the shapes that show halves.

Making halves

Cut out the four-strip. 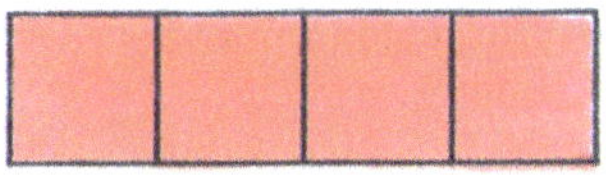

Fold it in half. 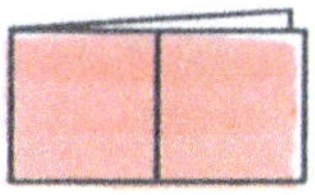

One half of 4 is ___ .

Cut out the six-strip. 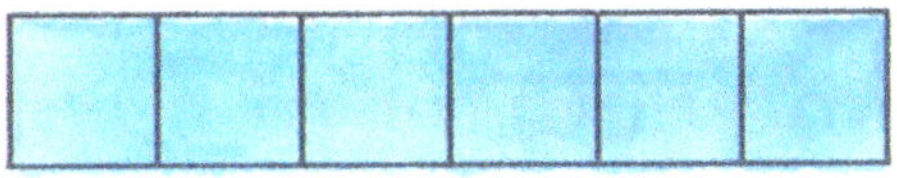

Fold it in half.

One half of 6 is ___ .

Make a tower with 8 cubes.

Halve it like this → 

One half of 8 is ___ .

Use 10 cubes.

One half of 10 is ___ .

Use cubes. One half of 12 is ___ .

One half of 16 is ___ .

One half of 20 is ___ .

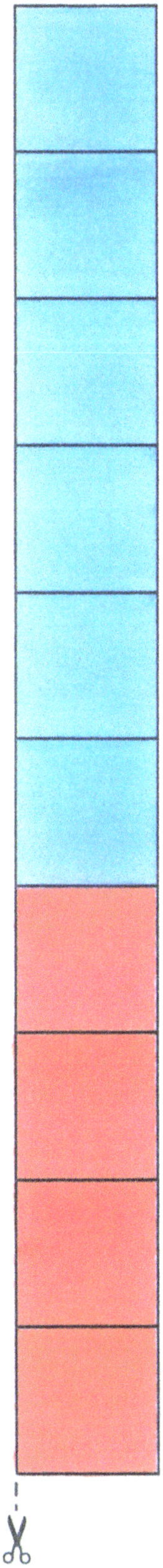

Quarters

You need

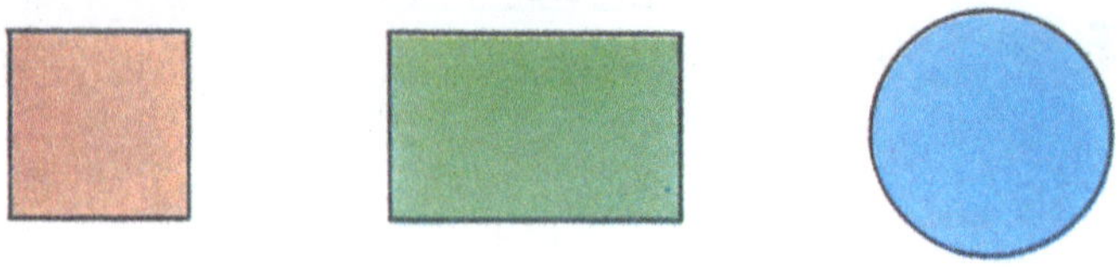

Fold each in quarters.

Colour one quarter of each shape.

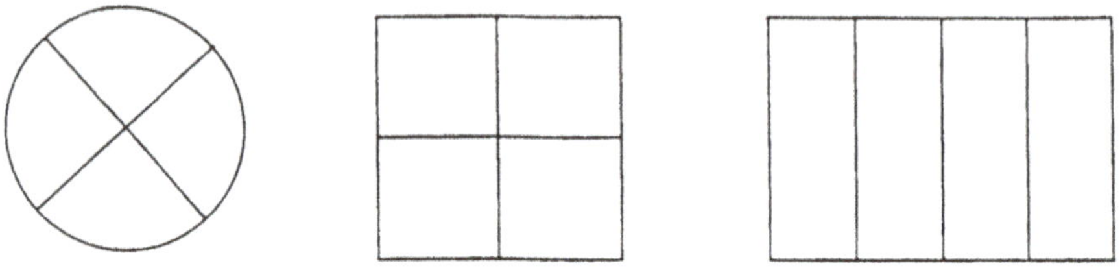

Tick the shapes that show quarters.

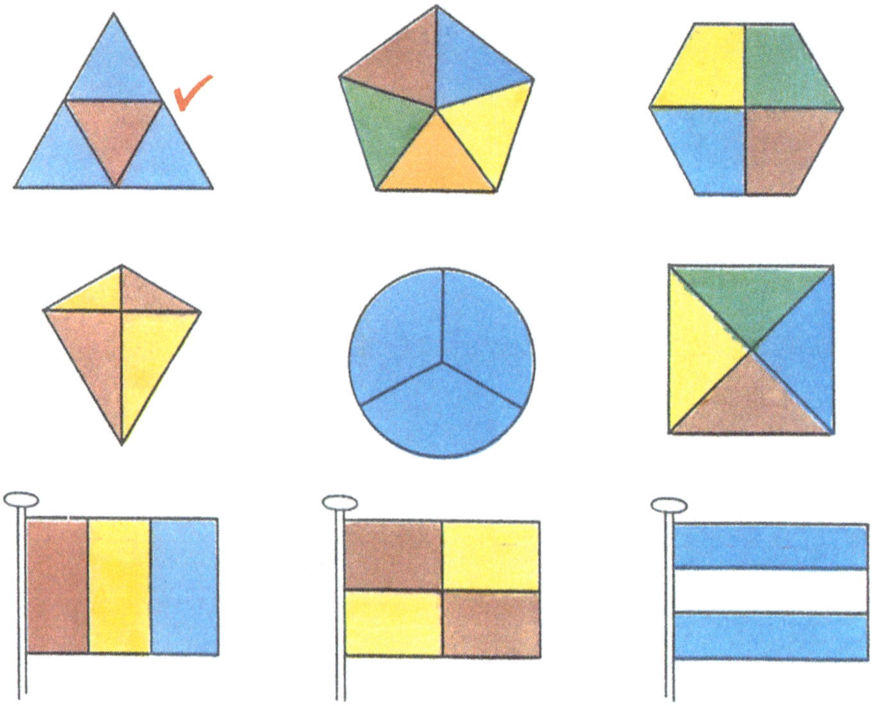

1	2	3	4	5	6	7	8	9	10	11	12	13	14	15	16	17	18	19	20	21	22	23

Heinemann is an imprint of Pearson Education Limited, a company incorporated in England and Wales, having its registered office at Edinburgh Gate, Harlow, Essex, CM20 2JE. Registered company number: 872828
ISBN 978 0 435 03094 0

First published 1991. Revised edition 1995. 19 28
Typeset and Illustrated by Oxprint Design. Printed and bound in Great Britain

ISBN 978-0-435030-94-0

SPMG

HEINEMANN MATHEMATICS 2

Name

WORKBOOK 4

Addition and Subtraction to 13, Halves and Quarters

Revised

Islands

Use cubes to add.

- 8 + 6 ☐
- 8 + 9 ☐
- 10 + 9 ☐
- 7 + 5 ☐
- 6 + 9 ☐
- 8 + 3 ☐
- 9 + 7 ☐
- 10 + 10 ☐
- 9 + 9 ☐
- 4 + 9 ☐

Use pennies. How much is it to go to

Mango Island and Nim-Nam-Noo ☐ p

Nim-Nam-Noo and Bear Island ☐ p ?

Use cubes to subtract. Match each boat to an island.

Write a subtraction story on this boat.

Extension

Amy has 13p

Jack has 11p

Amy and Jack go to Mango Island.
How much has each left?

Amy ___ p

Jack ___ p

To land on the island, find numbers which add to 11.

Use counters.

10 + 1				

How many birds? ___
3 fly away.

11 – 3 = ___

How many mangoes? ___
7 fall off.

11 – 7 = ___

How many flowers? ___
5 are picked.

11 – 5 = ___

How many hedgehogs? ___
9 hide.

11 – 9 = ___

Bushes

Each bush has 11 flowers. Write stories.

9 + 2 = 11

2 + 9 = 11

11 − 2 = 9

11 − 9 = 2

8 + 3 =

3 + 8 =

11 − 3 =

11 − 8 =

7 + 4 =

4 + 7 =

11 − 4 =

11 − 7 =

6 + 5 =

5 + 6 =

11 − 5 =

11 − 6 =

Investigation

Find sets of 3 numbers which add to 11.

In the jungle

$\begin{array}{r} 4 \\ +7 \\ \hline \end{array}$ ___

$\begin{array}{r} 11 \\ -3 \\ \hline \end{array}$ ___

$\begin{array}{r} 3 \\ +8 \\ \hline \end{array}$ ___

$\begin{array}{r} 11 \\ -9 \\ \hline \end{array}$ ___

$\begin{array}{r} 11 \\ -6 \\ \hline \end{array}$ ___

11 – 4 = ___

11 – 8 = ___

5 + 6 = ___

11 – 2 = ___

11 – 1 = ___

The nest has 11 eggs.
4 fall out.

How many left? ___

11 flies
5 ants
How many more flies? ___

3 + 4 + 4 = ___

5 + 2 + 3 = ___

Food

Buying food

How much does each spend?

Each child has 11p. They buy these things.
How much has each left?

Problem solving

Spend 11p.
What 3 things will you buy?

Nim-Nam-Noo

Put 12 Nim-nams on the island like this.

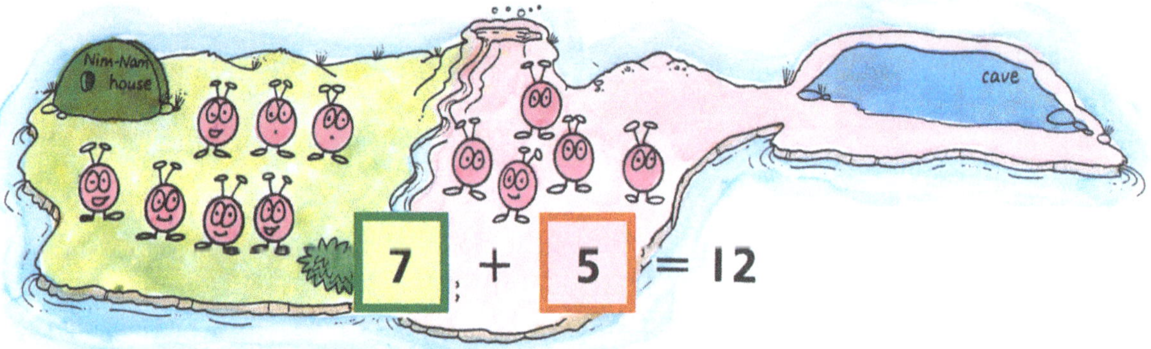

7 + 5 = 12

Find other ways to put 12 Nim-nams on the island.

□ + □ = 12

□ + □ = 12

□ + □ = 12

□ + □ = 12

□ + □ = 12

□ + □ = 12

□ + □ = 12

□ + □ = 12

Put 12 Nim-nams on the island like this.

5 + 4 + 3 = 12

Find other ways.

□ + □ + □ = 12

□ + □ + □ = 12

□ + □ + □ = 12

Put 12 Nim-nams on the island.

If Noo eats 5, how many are left?

12 − 5 = □

12 − 9 = □ 12 − 4 = □ 12 − 10 = □

12 − 7 = □ 12 − 6 = □ 12 − 3 = □

Nim-nams

7 + 5 =

12 − 5 =

12 − 7 =

5 + 7 =

9 + 3 =

3 + 9 =

12 − 3 =

12 − 9 =

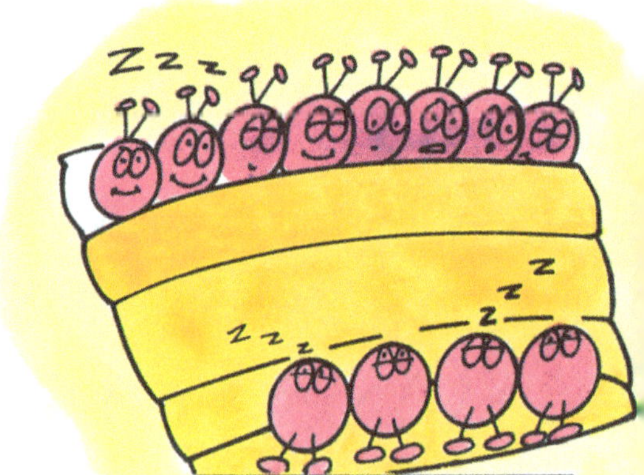

6 + 6 =

12 − 6 =

8 + 4 =

4 + 8 =

12 − 4 =

12 − 8 =

Nim-nam house

Find the answers. Colour them.

red	7 + 3	12 − 10	12 − 7
blue	12 − 4	8 + 3	6 + 6
green	6 + 3	12 − 9	12 − 8

How many altogether?

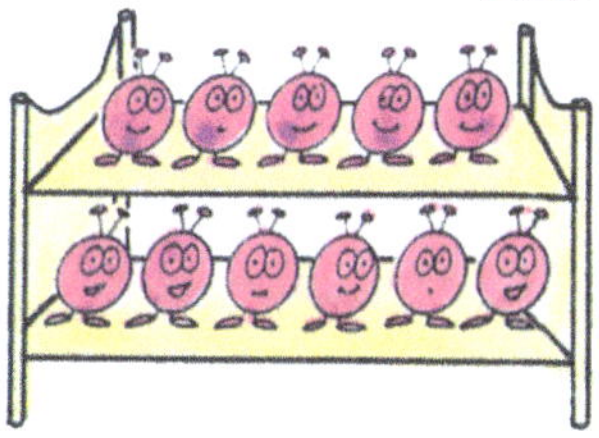

$\begin{array}{r} 5 \\ +6 \\ \hline \end{array}$ $\begin{array}{r} 8 \\ +4 \\ \hline \end{array}$ $\begin{array}{r} 7 \\ +5 \\ \hline \end{array}$ $\begin{array}{r} 3 \\ +9 \\ \hline \end{array}$

$\begin{array}{r} 5 \\ +7 \\ \hline \end{array}$ $\begin{array}{r} 6 \\ +6 \\ \hline \end{array}$ $\begin{array}{r} 3 \\ 4 \\ +5 \\ \hline \end{array}$ $\begin{array}{r} 6 \\ 4 \\ +2 \\ \hline \end{array}$ $\begin{array}{r} 4 \\ 4 \\ +3 \\ \hline \end{array}$

Bear Island

In each cave,
colour three bears that add to make 12.

The school cave has

an even answer greater than 10.

Write School above the school cave.

Extension

Use these numbers to make the sums.

9 8 4 3

8 + 4 = 12	+ ___ = 11	+ ___ = 12	+ ___ = 13
− ___ = 4	− ___ = 6	− ___ = 1	− ___ = 5

Use 13 counters.

$$\begin{array}{r} 6 \\ +7 \\ \hline \\ \hline \end{array}$$

$$\begin{array}{r} \\ + \\ \hline \\ \hline \end{array}$$

Find other stories for 13.

+ ___ 13	+ ___ 13	+ ___ 13	+ ___ 13	+ ___ 13	+ ___ 13

$2 + 3 + 8 = 13$

Find more stories like this for 13.

6 + 7 = 13

7 + 6 =

13 – 6 =

13 – 7 =

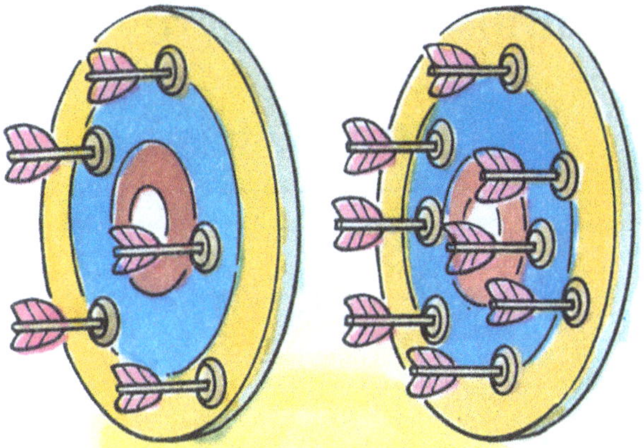

5 + 8 =

8 + 5 =

13 – 5 =

13 – 8 =

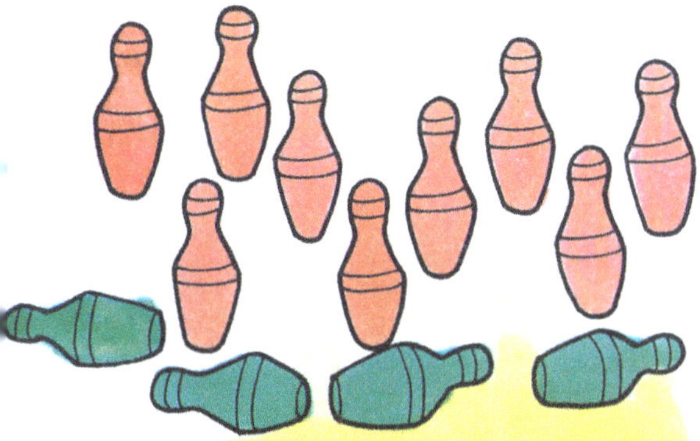

9 + 4 =

4 + 9 =

13 – 9 =

13 – 4 =

10 + 3 =

3 + 10 =

13 – 10 =

13 – 3 =

R24

Train ride

Colour a carriage to match each answer.

Spooky Castle

Write the missing number.

This key opens the door.

Cross out flies to make 13.

13 children go in.
8 come out.

How many are still in? ____

Add to find the one that is different. ✓

The trapdoor key is in it.

Escape

Write the answers.

7 + 6 =

4 + 8 =

12 – 3 =

13 – 4 =

11 – 9 =

7 + 4 =

11 – 4 =

12 – 6 =

13 – 6 =

Colour the boxes

blue if the answer is odd,

red if the answer is even.

5	12	9	8	7	13
+8	–9	+4	+5	+5	–8
___	___	___	___	___	___

Which door has an even answer? Colour it red.

Problem solving

Amy had 13p.
She lost 7p in the sea.

How much is left? ___ p

Colour the monster that has two more black spots than green spots.

Find chests with the same answer.
Colour them to match.

The treasure is in the white chest.
Mark it ✗.

Stickers

Problem solving / Extension

Find the cost of a fox and a bear. ____

Find the cost of a fox, a tiger and a dog. ____

I spend 13p.
I buy 2 animals.
What do I buy? ____________

I have 8p.
I want a panda.
How much more do I need? ____

I have 12p. I buy a bear.
What else can I now buy?

fox or ________ or ________

Prizes

8. [+] [7] [=] ☐

15. [−] [6] [=] ☐

Now do these.

7 + 9 = ☐ 6 + 8 = ☐ 10 + 9 = ☐

16 − 7 = ☐ 14 − 8 = ☐ 17 − 9 = ☐

Who wins a prize? (✓)

[4] [+] [8] [+] [3] [+] [4] [=] ____

[9] [+] [2] [+] [5] [+] [2] [=] ____

[8] [+] [6] [+] [7] [−] [2] [=] ____

Halves

You need

Fold each in half.

Colour one half of each shape.

Tick the shapes that show halves.

Making halves

Cut out the four-strip.

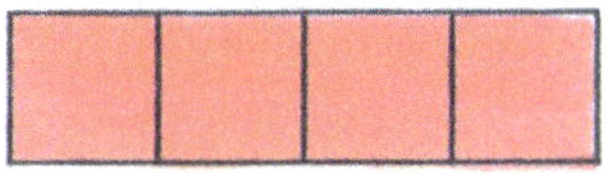

Fold it in half.

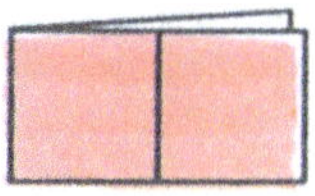

One half of 4 is ___ .

Cut out the six-strip.

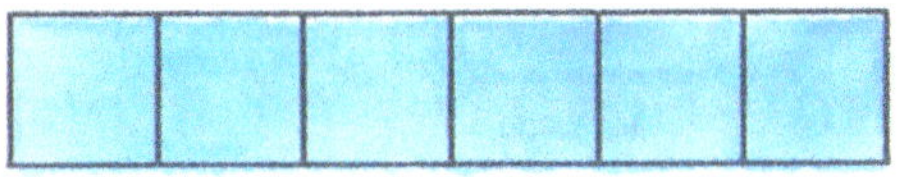

Fold it in half.

One half of 6 is ___ .

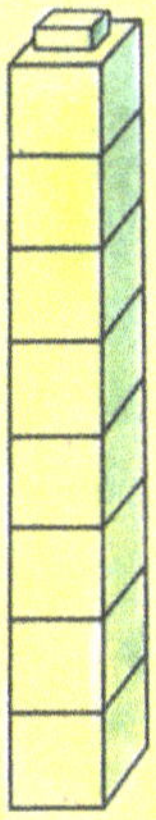

Make a tower with 8 cubes.

Halve it like this →

One half of 8 is ___ .

Use 10 cubes.

One half of 10 is ___ .

Use cubes. One half of 12 is ___ .

One half of 16 is ___ .

One half of 20 is ___ .

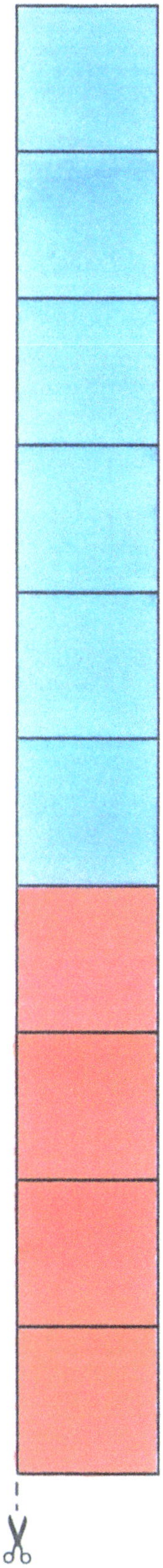

Quarters

You need

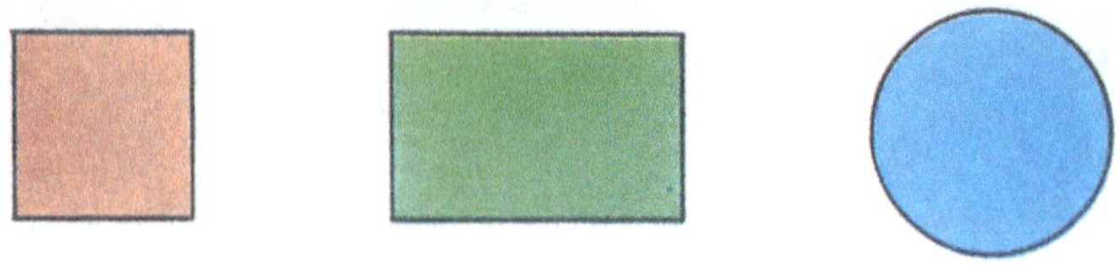

Fold each in quarters.

Colour one quarter of each shape.

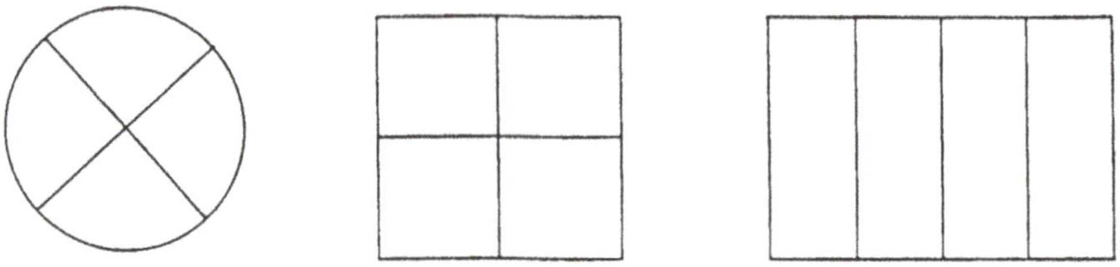

Tick the shapes that show quarters.

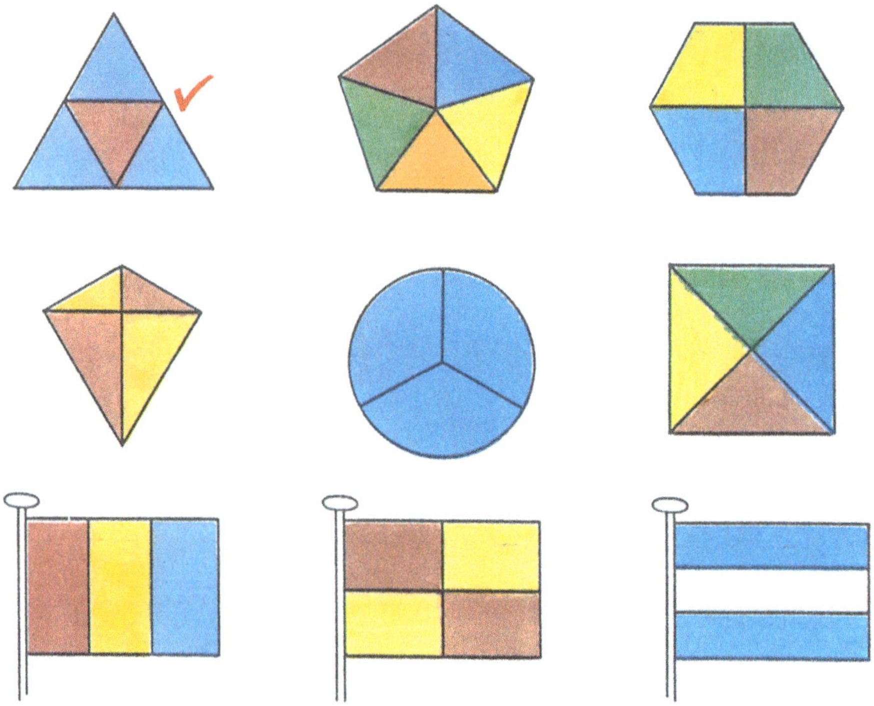

1	2	3	4	5	6	7	8	9	10	11	12	13	14	15	16	17	18	19	20	21	22	23

Heinemann is an imprint of Pearson Education Limited, a company incorporated in England and Wales, having its registered office at Edinburgh Gate, Harlow, Essex, CM20 2JE. Registered company number: 872828
ISBN 978 0 435 03094 0
First published 1991. Revised edition 1995. 19 28
Typeset and Illustrated by Oxprint Design. Printed and bound in Great Britain

ISBN 978-0-435030-94-0

SPMG

HEINEMANN MATHEMATICS 2

Name

WORKBOOK 4

Addition and Subtraction to 13, Halves and Quarters

Islands

Use cubes to add.

Use pennies. How much is it to go to

Mango Island and Nim-Nam-Noo ☐ p

Nim-Nam-Noo and Bear Island ☐ p ?

Use cubes to subtract. Match each boat to an island.

Write a subtraction story on this boat.

Extension

Amy and Jack go to Mango Island.
How much has each left?

Amy ___ p

Jack ___ p

To land on the island, find numbers which add to 11.

Use counters.

10 + 1				

How many ? ___
3 fly away.

11 − 3 = ___

How many ? ___
5 are picked.

11 − 5 = ___

How many ? ___
7 fall off.

11 − 7 = ___

How many ? ___
9 hide.

11 − 9 = ___

Bushes

Each bush has 11 flowers. Write stories.

9 + 2 = 11

2 + 9 = 11

11 – 2 = 9

11 – 9 = 2

8 + 3 =

3 + 8 =

11 – 3 =

11 – 8 =

7 + 4 =

4 + 7 =

11 – 4 =

11 – 7 =

6 + 5 =

5 + 6 =

11 – 5 =

11 – 6 =

Investigation

Find sets of 3 numbers which add to 11.

In the jungle

4 + 7 = ___ ___

11 − 3 = ___ ___

3 + 8 = ___ ___

11 − 9 = ___ ___

11 − 6 = ___ ___

11 − 4 = ___

11 − 8 = ___

5 + 6 = ___

11 − 2 = ___

11 − 1 = ___

The nest has 11 eggs.
4 fall out.

How many left? ___

11 flies
5 ants
How many more flies? ___

3 + 4 + 4 = ___

5 + 2 + 3 = ___

Buying food

How much does each spend?

☐ p ☐ p ☐ p

Each child has 11p. They buy these things.
How much has each left?

___ p ___ p ___ p

Spend 11p.
What 3 things will you buy?

Nim-Nam-Noo

Put 12 Nim-nams on the island like this.

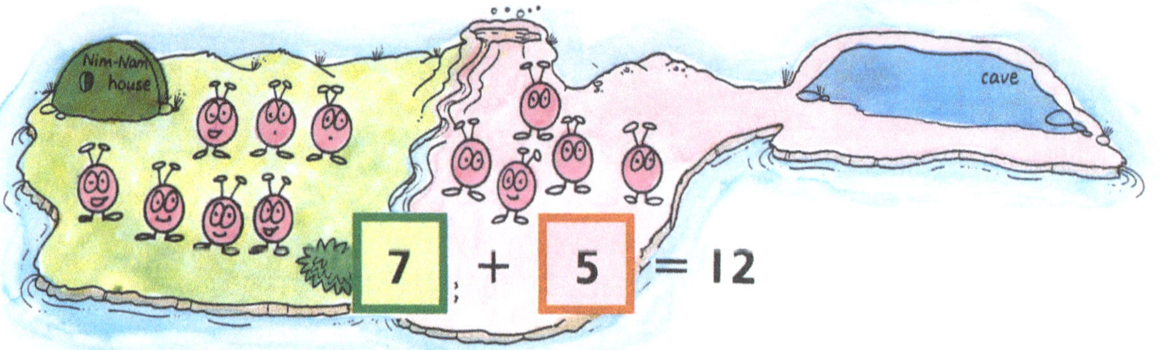

7 + 5 = 12

Find other ways to put 12 Nim-nams on the island.

☐	+	☐	=	12	☐	+	☐	=	12
☐	+	☐	=	12	☐	+	☐	=	12
☐	+	☐	=	12	☐	+	☐	=	12
☐	+	☐	=	12	☐	+	☐	=	12

Put 12 Nim-nams on the island like this.

5 + 4 + 3 = 12

Find other ways.

☐ + ☐ + ☐ = 12

☐ + ☐ + ☐ = 12

☐ + ☐ + ☐ = 12

Put 12 Nim-nams on the island.

If Noo eats 5, how many are left?

12 – 5 = ☐

12 – 9 = ☐   12 – 4 = ☐   12 – 10 = ☐

12 – 7 = ☐   12 – 6 = ☐   12 – 3 = ☐

Nim-nams

7 + 5 =

12 − 5 =

12 − 7 =

5 + 7 =

9 + 3 =

3 + 9 =

12 − 3 =

12 − 9 =

6 + 6 =

12 − 6 =

8 + 4 =

4 + 8 =

12 − 4 =

12 − 8 =

Nim-nam house

Find the answers. Colour them.

red	7 + 3	12 – 10	12 – 7
blue	12 – 4	8 + 3	6 + 6
green	6 + 3	12 – 9	12 – 8

How many altogether?

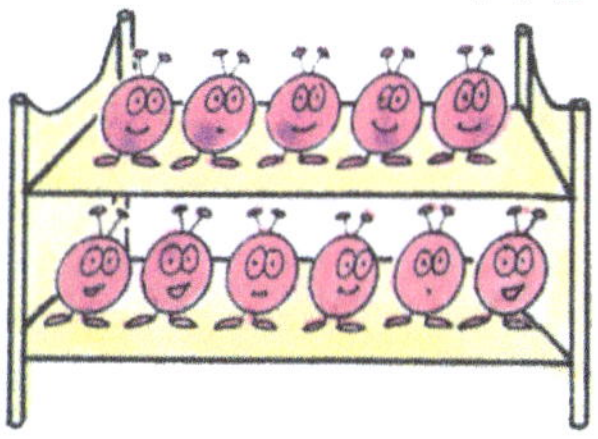

$\begin{array}{r} 5 \\ +6 \\ \hline \end{array}$ $\begin{array}{r} 8 \\ +4 \\ \hline \end{array}$ $\begin{array}{r} 7 \\ +5 \\ \hline \end{array}$ $\begin{array}{r} 3 \\ +9 \\ \hline \end{array}$

$\begin{array}{r} 5 \\ +7 \\ \hline \end{array}$ $\begin{array}{r} 6 \\ +6 \\ \hline \end{array}$ $\begin{array}{r} 3 \\ 4 \\ +5 \\ \hline \end{array}$ $\begin{array}{r} 6 \\ 4 \\ +2 \\ \hline \end{array}$ $\begin{array}{r} 4 \\ 4 \\ +3 \\ \hline \end{array}$

Bear Island

In each cave,
colour three bears that add to make 12.

The school cave has

an even answer greater than 10.

Write **School** above the school cave.

Use these numbers to make the sums.

9 **8** **4** **3**

$$\begin{array}{r} 8 \\ +\ 4 \\ \hline 12 \\ \hline \end{array} \qquad \begin{array}{r} \\ +\ \ \\ \hline 11 \\ \hline \end{array} \qquad \begin{array}{r} \\ +\ \ \\ \hline 12 \\ \hline \end{array} \qquad \begin{array}{r} \\ +\ \ \\ \hline 13 \\ \hline \end{array}$$

$$\begin{array}{r} \\ -\ \ \\ \hline 4 \\ \hline \end{array} \qquad \begin{array}{r} \\ -\ \ \\ \hline 6 \\ \hline \end{array} \qquad \begin{array}{r} \\ -\ \ \\ \hline 1 \\ \hline \end{array} \qquad \begin{array}{r} \\ -\ \ \\ \hline 5 \\ \hline \end{array}$$

Fun Island

Use 13 counters.

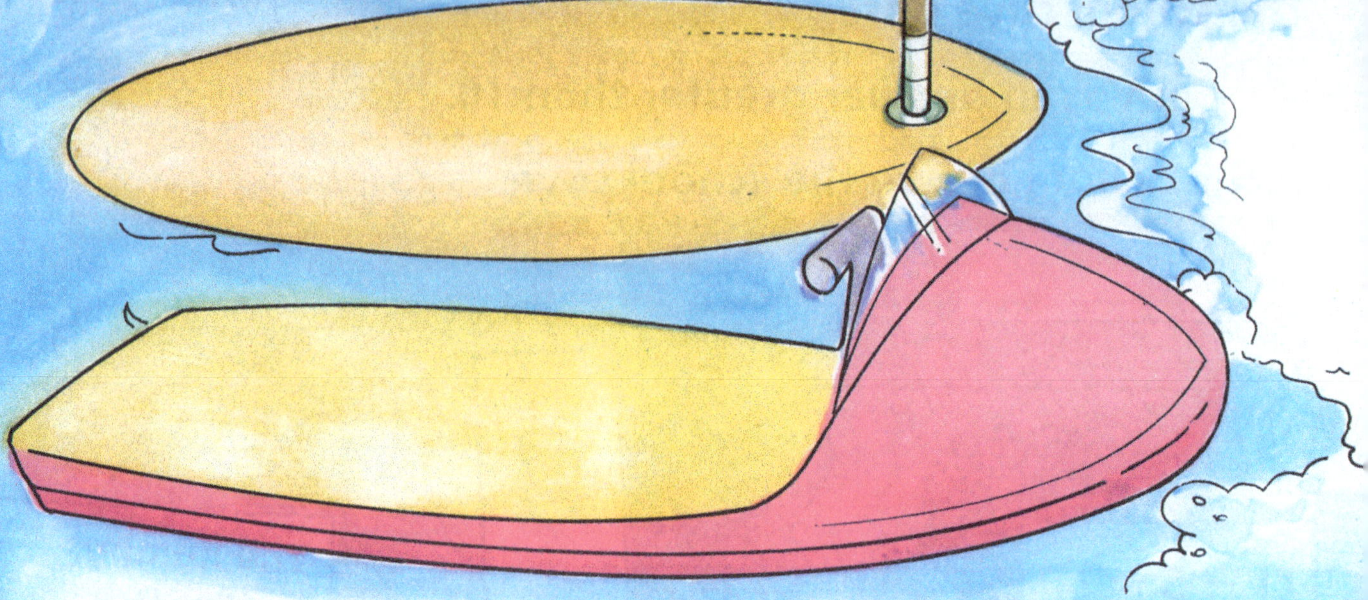

6
+7

+

Find other stories for 13.

+	+	+	+	+	+
13	13	13	13	13	13

2 + 3 + 8 = 13

Find more stories like this for 13.

$6 + 7 = 13$

$7 + 6 =$

$13 - 6 =$

$13 - 7 =$

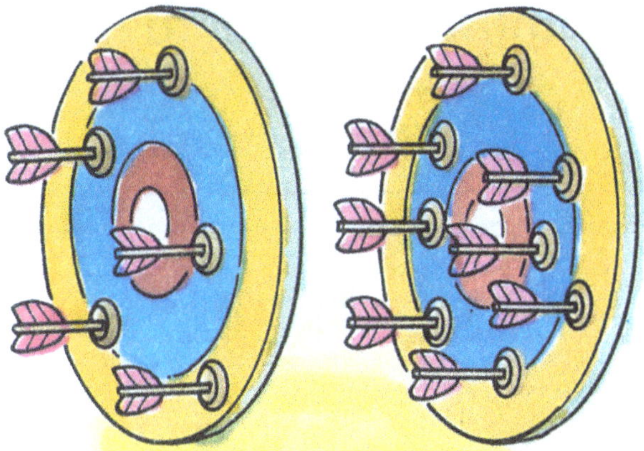

$5 + 8 =$

$8 + 5 =$

$13 - 5 =$

$13 - 8 =$

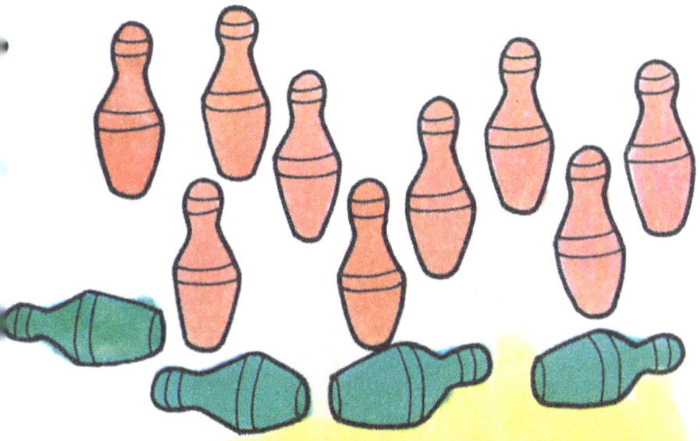

$9 + 4 =$

$4 + 9 =$

$13 - 9 =$

$13 - 4 =$

$10 + 3 =$

$3 + 10 =$

$13 - 10 =$

$13 - 3 =$

R 24

Train ride

Colour a carriage to match each answer.

Spooky Castle

Write the missing number.

This key opens the door.

Cross out flies to make 13.

13 children go in.
8 come out.

How many are still in? ____

Add to find the one that is different. 

The trapdoor key is in it.

Escape

Write the answers.

7 + 6 =

4 + 8 =

12 – 3 =

13 – 4 =

11 – 9 =

7 + 4 =

11 – 4 =

12 – 6 =

13 – 6 =

Colour the boxes

blue if the answer is odd,

red if the answer is even.

5	12	9	8	7	13
+8	–9	+4	+5	+5	–8

Which door has an even answer? Colour it red.

Problem solving

Amy had 13p.
She lost 7p in the sea.

How much is left? ___ p

Colour the monster that has two more black spots than green spots.

Find chests with the same answer.
Colour them to match.

The treasure is in the white chest.
Mark it ✗.

Stickers

Problem solving/Extension

Find the cost of a fox and a bear. ____

Find the cost of a fox, a tiger and a dog. ____

I spend 13p.
I buy 2 animals.
What do I buy? ____________

I have 8p.
I want a panda.
How much more do I need? ____

I have 12p. I buy a bear.
What else can I now buy?

fox or ________ or ________

Prizes

8. [+] [7] [=] ____

15. [−] [6] [=] ____

Now do these.

7 + 9 = ☐	6 + 8 = ☐	10 + 9 = ☐
16 − 7 = ☐	14 − 8 = ☐	17 − 9 = ☐

Who wins a prize? (✓)

[4] [+] [8] [+] [3] [+] [4] [=] ____

[9] [+] [2] [+] [5] [+] [2] [=] ____

[8] [+] [6] [+] [7] [−] [2] [=] ____

Halves

You need

Fold each in half.

Colour one half of each shape.

Tick the shapes that show halves.

Making halves

Cut out the four-strip.

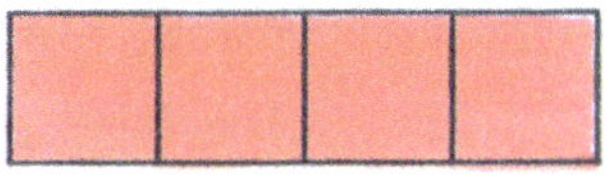

Fold it in half.

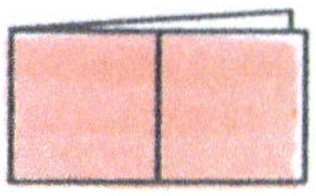

One half of 4 is ___ .

Cut out the six-strip.

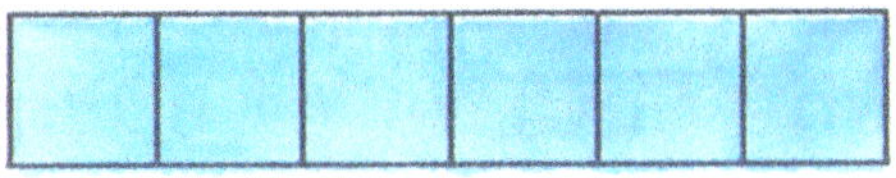

Fold it in half.

One half of 6 is ___ .

Make a tower with 8 cubes.

Halve it like this →

One half of 8 is ___ .

Use 10 cubes.

One half of 10 is ___ .

Use cubes. One half of 12 is ___ .

One half of 16 is ___ .

One half of 20 is ___ .

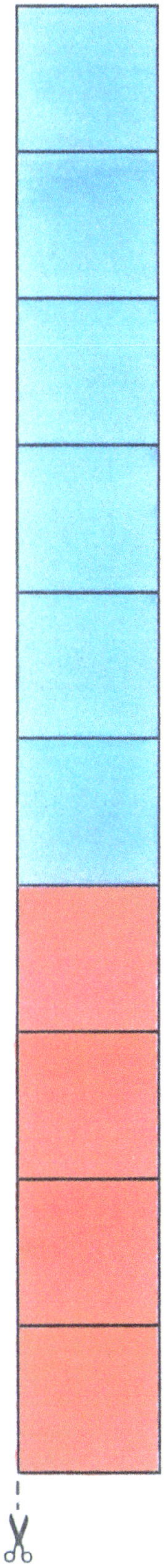

Quarters

You need

Fold each in quarters.

Colour one quarter of each shape.

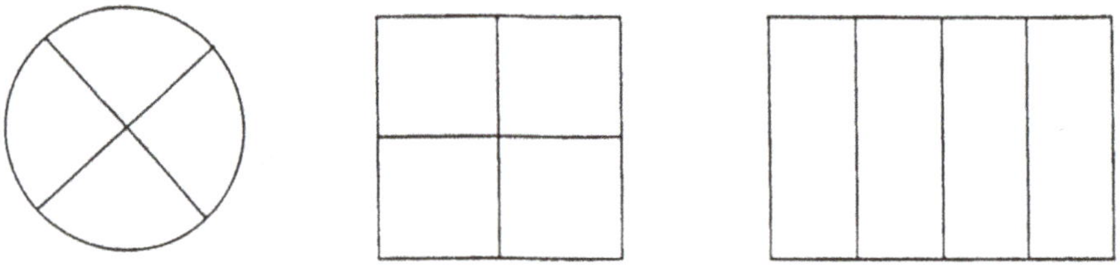

Tick the shapes that show quarters.

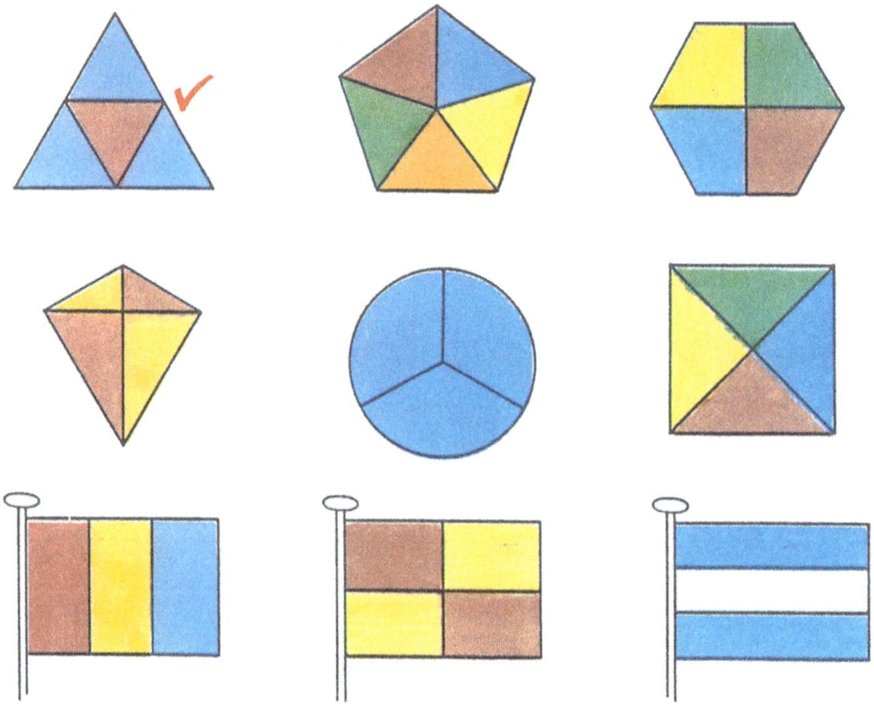

1	2	3	4	5	6	7	8	9	10	11	12	13	14	15	16	17	18	19	20	21	22	23

Heinemann is an imprint of Pearson Education Limited, a company incorporated in England and Wales, having its registered office at Edinburgh Gate, Harlow, Essex, CM20 2JE. Registered company number: 872828
ISBN 978 0 435 03094 0
First published 1991. Revised edition 1995. 19 28
Typeset and Illustrated by Oxprint Design. Printed and bound in Great Britain

ISBN 978-0-435030-94-0

HEINEMANN MATHEMATICS 2

Name

WORKBOOK 4

Addition and Subtraction to 13, Halves and Quarters

Revised

Islands

Use cubes to add.

Use pennies. How much is it to go to

Mango Island and Nim-Nam-Noo ☐ p

Nim-Nam-Noo and Bear Island ☐ p ?

Use cubes to subtract. Match each boat to an island.

Write a subtraction story on this boat.

Extension

Amy and Jack go to Mango Island.
How much has each left?

Amy ___ p

Jack ___ p

To land on the island, find numbers which add to 11.

Use counters.

10 + 1				

How many birds? ___
3 fly away.

11 − 3 = ___

How many mangoes? ___
7 fall off.

11 − 7 = ___

How many flowers? ___
5 are picked.

11 − 5 = ___

How many hedgehogs? ___
9 hide.

11 − 9 = ___

Bushes

Each bush has 11 flowers. Write stories.

9 + 2 = 11

2 + 9 = 11

11 – 2 = 9

11 – 9 = 2

8 + 3 =

3 + 8 =

11 – 3 =

11 – 8 =

7 + 4 =

4 + 7 =

11 – 4 =

11 – 7 =

6 + 5 =

5 + 6 =

11 – 5 =

11 – 6 =

Investigation

Find sets of 3 numbers which add to 11.

In the jungle

$4 + 7 =$ ___

$11 - 3 =$ ___

$3 + 8 =$ ___

$11 - 9 =$ ___

$11 - 6 =$ ___

$11 - 4 =$ ___

$11 - 8 =$ ___

$5 + 6 =$ ___

$11 - 2 =$ ___

$11 - 1 =$ ___

The nest has 11 eggs.
4 fall out.

How many left? ___

11 flies
5 ants
How many more flies? ___

$3 + 4 + 4 =$ ___

$5 + 2 + 3 =$ ___

Buying food

How much does each spend?

☐ p

☐ p

☐ p

Each child has 11p. They buy these things.
How much has each left?

___ p

___ p

___ p

Spend 11p.
What 3 things will you buy?

Nim-Nam-Noo

Put 12 Nim-nams on the island like this.

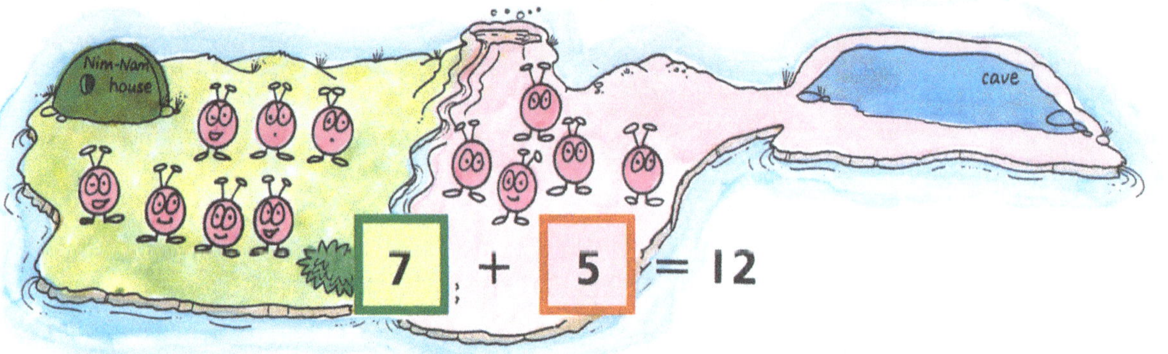

7 + 5 = 12

Find other ways to put 12 Nim-nams on the island.

□ + □ = 12   □ + □ = 12

□ + □ = 12   □ + □ = 12

□ + □ = 12   □ + □ = 12

□ + □ = 12   □ + □ = 12

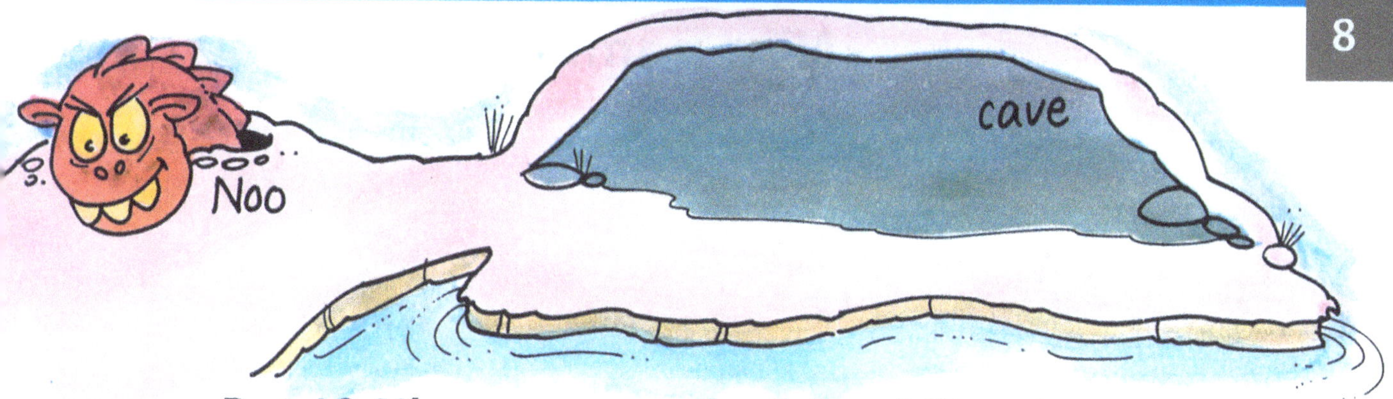

Put 12 Nim-nams on the island like this.

5 + **4** + **3** = 12

Find other ways.

□ + □ + □ = 12

□ + □ + □ = 12

□ + □ + □ = 12

Put 12 Nim-nams on the island.

If Noo eats 5, how many are left?

12 – 5 = □

12 – 9 = □

12 – 4 = □

12 – 10 = □

12 – 7 = □

12 – 6 = □

12 – 3 = □

Nim-nams

7 + 5 =

12 – 5 =

12 – 7 =

5 + 7 =

9 + 3 =

3 + 9 =

12 – 3 =

12 – 9 =

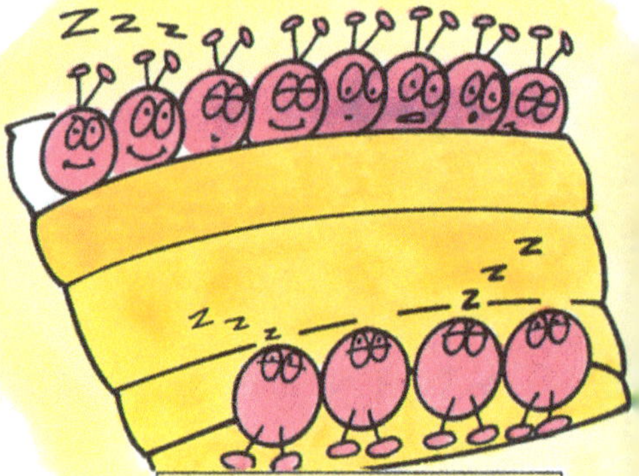

6 + 6 =

12 – 6 =

8 + 4 =

4 + 8 =

12 – 4 =

12 – 8 =

Nim-nam house

Find the answers. Colour them.

red	7 + 3	12 − 10	12 − 7
blue	12 − 4	8 + 3	6 + 6
green	6 + 3	12 − 9	12 − 8

How many altogether?

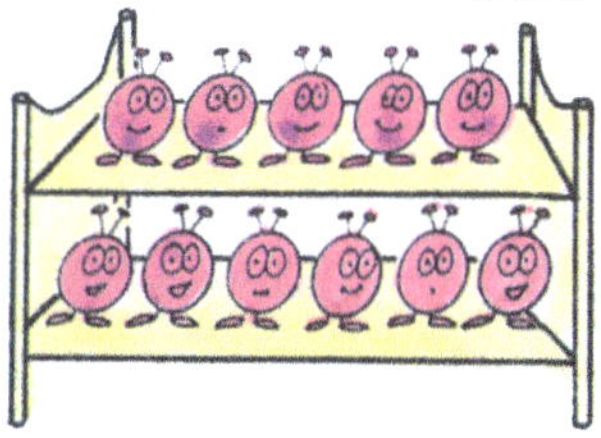

5	8	7	3
+6	+4	+5	+9
___	___	___	___

		3	6	4
5	6	4	4	4
+7	+6	+5	+2	+3
___	___	___	___	___

Bear Island

In each cave,
colour three bears that add to make 12.

The school cave has

an even answer greater than 10.

Write School above the school cave.

Extension

Use these numbers to make the sums.

9 8 4 3

8 + 4 = 12	+ ___ = 11	+ ___ = 12	+ ___ = 13
− ___ = 4	− ___ = 6	− ___ = 1	− ___ = 5

Fun Island

Use 13 counters.

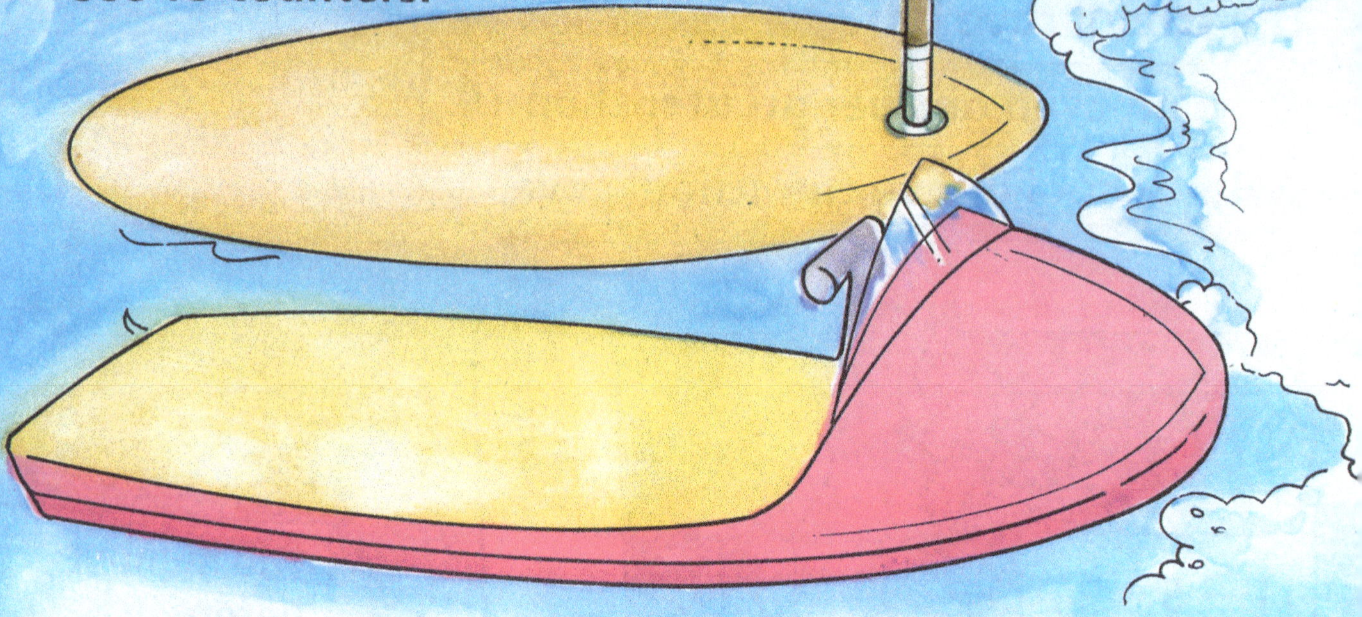

6
+7
___

___

\+
___

___

Find other stories for 13.

+	+	+	+	+	+
13	13	13	13	13	13

2 + 3 + 8 = 13

Find more stories like this for 13.

6 + 7 = 13

7 + 6 =

13 − 6 =

13 − 7 =

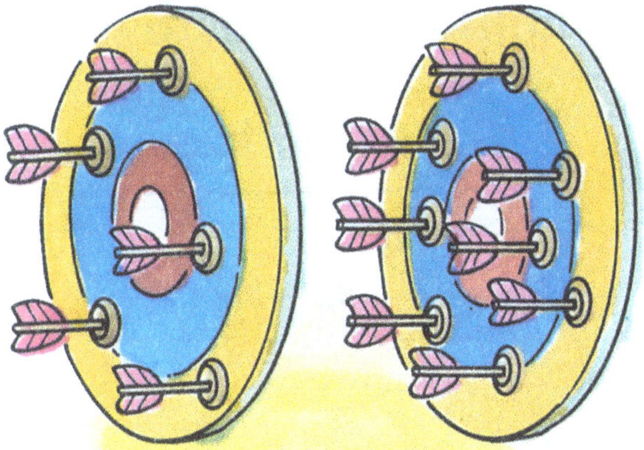

5 + 8 =

8 + 5 =

13 − 5 =

13 − 8 =

9 + 4 =

4 + 9 =

13 − 9 =

13 − 4 =

10 + 3 =

3 + 10 =

13 − 10 =

13 − 3 =

R24

Train ride

Colour a carriage to match each answer.

Spooky Castle

Write the missing number.

This key opens the door.

Cross out flies to make 13.

13 children go in.
8 come out.

How many are still in? ____

Add to find the one that is different.

The trapdoor key is in it.

Escape

Write the answers.

$7 + 6 =$

$4 + 8 =$

$12 - 3 =$

$13 - 4 =$

$11 - 9 =$

$7 + 4 =$

$11 - 4 =$

$12 - 6 =$

$13 - 6 =$

Colour the boxes

blue if the answer is odd,

red if the answer is even.

5	12	9	8	7	13
+8	−9	+4	+5	+5	−8
___	___	___	___	___	___

Which door has an even answer? Colour it red.

Problem solving

Amy had 13p.
She lost 7p in the sea.

How much is left? ___ p

Colour the monster that has **two more** black spots than green spots.

Find chests with the same answer.
Colour them to match.

The treasure is in the white chest.
Mark it ✗.

Stickers

Problem solving / Extension

Find the cost of a fox and a bear. ____

Find the cost of a fox, a tiger and a dog. ____

I spend 13p.
I buy 2 animals.
What do I buy? ____________

I have 8p.
I want a panda.
How much more do I need? ____

I have 12p. I buy a bear.
What else can I now buy?

fox or ________ or ________

Prizes

8. [+] [7] [=] [ ]

15. [−] [6] [=] [ ]

Now do these.

7 + 9 = [ ] 6 + 8 = [ ] 10 + 9 = [ ]

16 − 7 = [ ] 14 − 8 = [ ] 17 − 9 = [ ]

Who wins a prize? (✓)

[4] [+] [8] [+] [3] [+] [4] [=] ____

[9] [+] [2] [+] [5] [+] [2] [=] ____

[8] [+] [6] [+] [7] [−] [2] [=] ____

Halves

You need

Fold each in half.

Colour one half of each shape.

Tick the shapes that show halves.

Making halves

Cut out the four-strip. 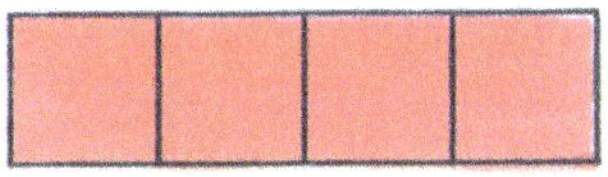

Fold it in half. 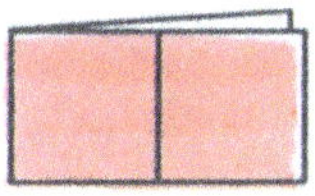

One half of 4 is ____ .

Cut out the six-strip. 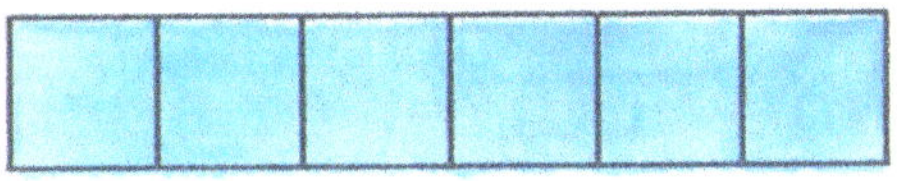

Fold it in half.

One half of 6 is ____ .

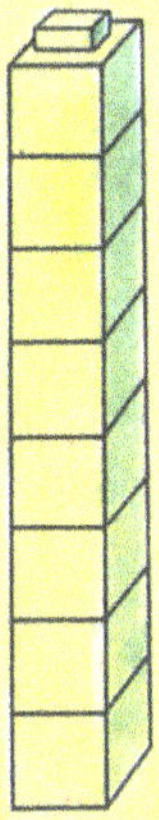

Make a tower with 8 cubes.

Halve it like this → 

One half of 8 is ____ .

Use 10 cubes.

One half of 10 is ____ .

Use cubes. One half of 12 is ____ .

One half of 16 is ____ .

One half of 20 is ____ .

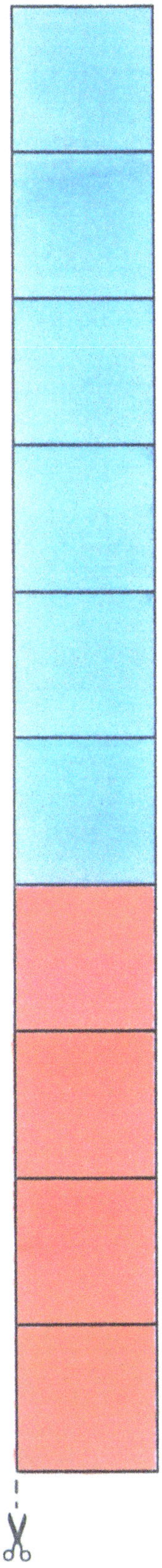

Quarters

You need

Fold each in quarters.

Colour one quarter of each shape.

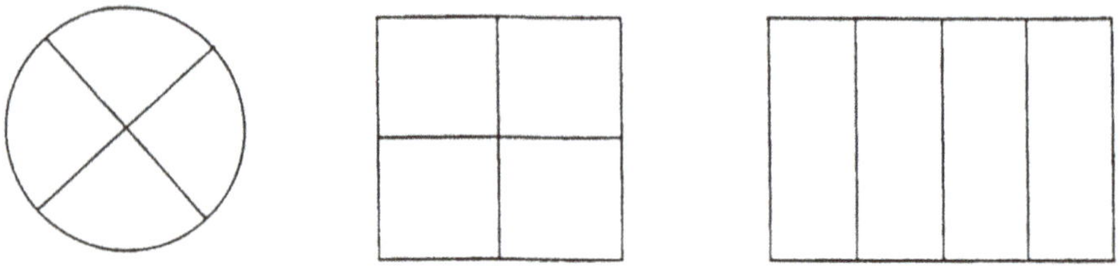

Tick the shapes that show quarters.

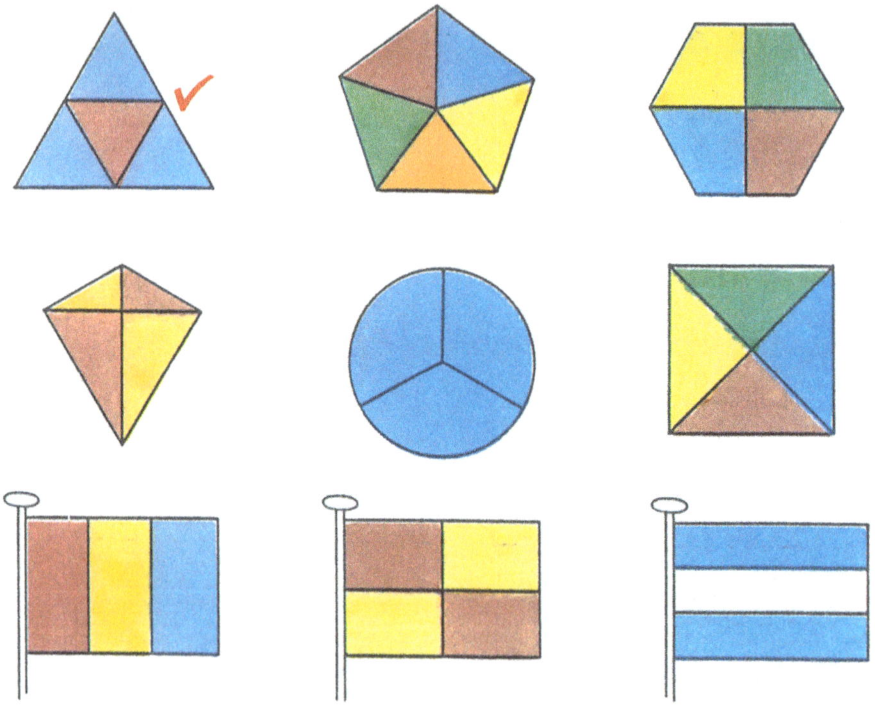

1	2	3	4	5	6	7	8	9	10	11	12	13	14	15	16	17	18	19	20	21	22	23

Heinemann is an imprint of Pearson Education Limited, a company incorporated in England and Wales, having its registered office at Edinburgh Gate, Harlow, Essex, CM20 2JE. Registered company number: 872828
ISBN 978 0 435 03094 0 © Scottish Primary Mathematics Group 1981.
First published 1991. Revised edition 1995. 19 28
Typeset and Illustrated by Oxprint Design. Printed and bound in Great Britain

ISBN 978-0-435030-94-0

SPMG

HEINEMANN MATHEMATICS 2

Name

WORKBOOK 4

Addition and Subtraction to 13, Halves and Quarters

Revised

Islands

Use cubes to add.

Use pennies. **How much is it to go to**

Mango Island and Nim-Nam-Noo ☐ **p**

Nim-Nam-Noo and Bear Island ☐ **p ?**

Use cubes to subtract. Match each boat to an island.

Write a subtraction story on this boat.

Extension

Amy and Jack go to Mango Island.
How much has each left?

Amy ____ p

Jack ____ p

To land on the island, find numbers which add to 11.

Use counters.

10 + 1				

How many ? ___
3 fly away.

11 − 3 = ___

How many ? ___
7 fall off.

11 − 7 = ___

How many ? ___
5 are picked.

11 − 5 = ___

How many ? ___
9 hide.

11 − 9 = ___

Bushes

Each bush has 11 flowers. Write stories.

9 + 2 = 11

2 + 9 = 11

11 – 2 = 9

11 – 9 = 2

8 + 3 =

3 + 8 =

11 – 3 =

11 – 8 =

7 + 4 =

4 + 7 =

11 – 4 =

11 – 7 =

6 + 5 =

5 + 6 =

11 – 5 =

11 – 6 =

Investigation

Find sets of 3 numbers which add to 11.

In the jungle

4	11	3	11	11
+7	−3	+8	−9	−6
___	___	___	___	___

11 − 8 = ___

11 − 4 = ___

5 + 6 = ___

11 − 2 = ___

11 − 1 = ___

The nest has 11 eggs.
4 fall out.

How many left? ___

11 flies
5 ants
How many more flies? ___

3 + 4 + 4 = ___

5 + 2 + 3 = ___

Food

Buying food

How much does each spend?

☐ p ☐ p ☐ p

Each child has 11p. They buy these things.
How much has each left?

___ p ___ p ___ p

Problem solving

Spend 11p.
What 3 things will you buy?

Nim-Nam-Noo

Put 12 Nim-nams on the island like this.

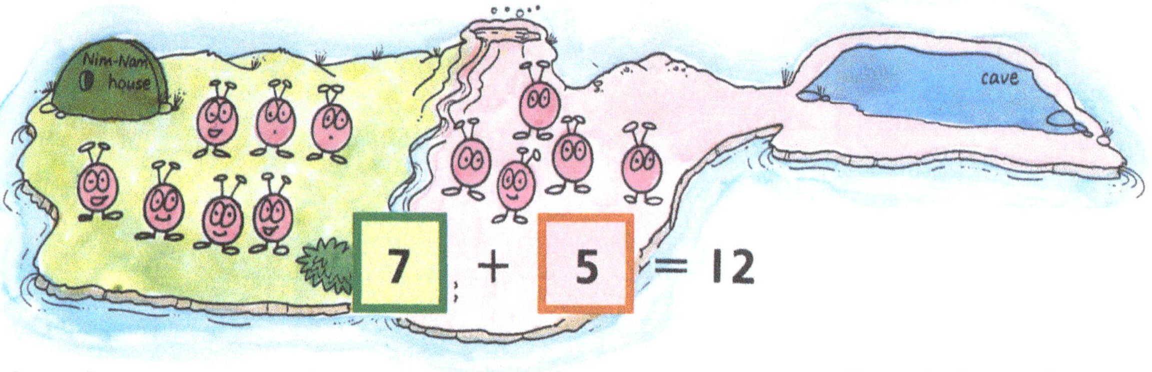

7 + 5 = 12

Find other ways to put 12 Nim-nams on the island.

☐ + ☐ = 12   ☐ + ☐ = 12

☐ + ☐ = 12   ☐ + ☐ = 12

☐ + ☐ = 12   ☐ + ☐ = 12

☐ + ☐ = 12   ☐ + ☐ = 12

Put 12 Nim-nams on the island like this.

5 + 4 + 3 = 12

Find other ways.

☐ + ☐ + ☐ = 12

☐ + ☐ + ☐ = 12

☐ + ☐ + ☐ = 12

Put 12 Nim-nams on the island.

If Noo eats 5, how many are left?

$12 - 5 =$ ☐

$12 - 9 =$ ☐ $12 - 4 =$ ☐ $12 - 10 =$ ☐

$12 - 7 =$ ☐ $12 - 6 =$ ☐ $12 - 3 =$ ☐

Nim-nams

7 + 5 =

12 − 5 =

12 − 7 =

5 + 7 =

9 + 3 =

3 + 9 =

12 − 3 =

12 − 9 =

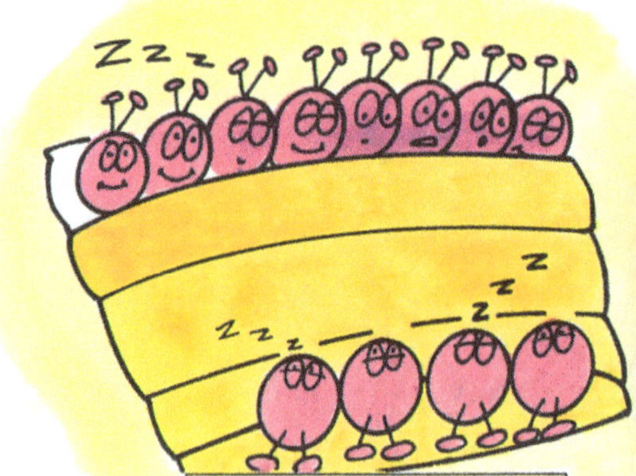

6 + 6 =

12 − 6 =

8 + 4 =

4 + 8 =

12 − 4 =

12 − 8 =

Nim-nam house

Find the answers. Colour them.

red	7 + 3	12 − 10	12 − 7
blue	12 − 4	8 + 3	6 + 6
green	6 + 3	12 − 9	12 − 8

How many altogether?

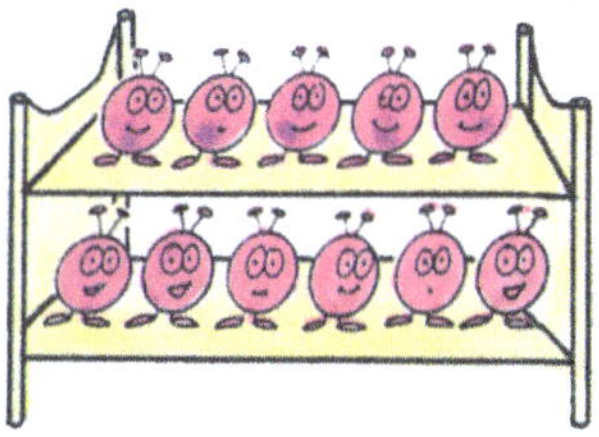

5	8	7	3
+6	+4	+5	+9
___	___	___	___

		3	6	4
5	6	4	4	4
+7	+6	+5	+2	+3
___	___	___	___	___

Bear Island

In each cave,
colour three bears that add to make 12.

The school cave has

an even answer greater than 10.

Write School above the school cave.

Extension

Use these numbers to make the sums.

9 8 4 3

Fun Island

Use 13 counters.

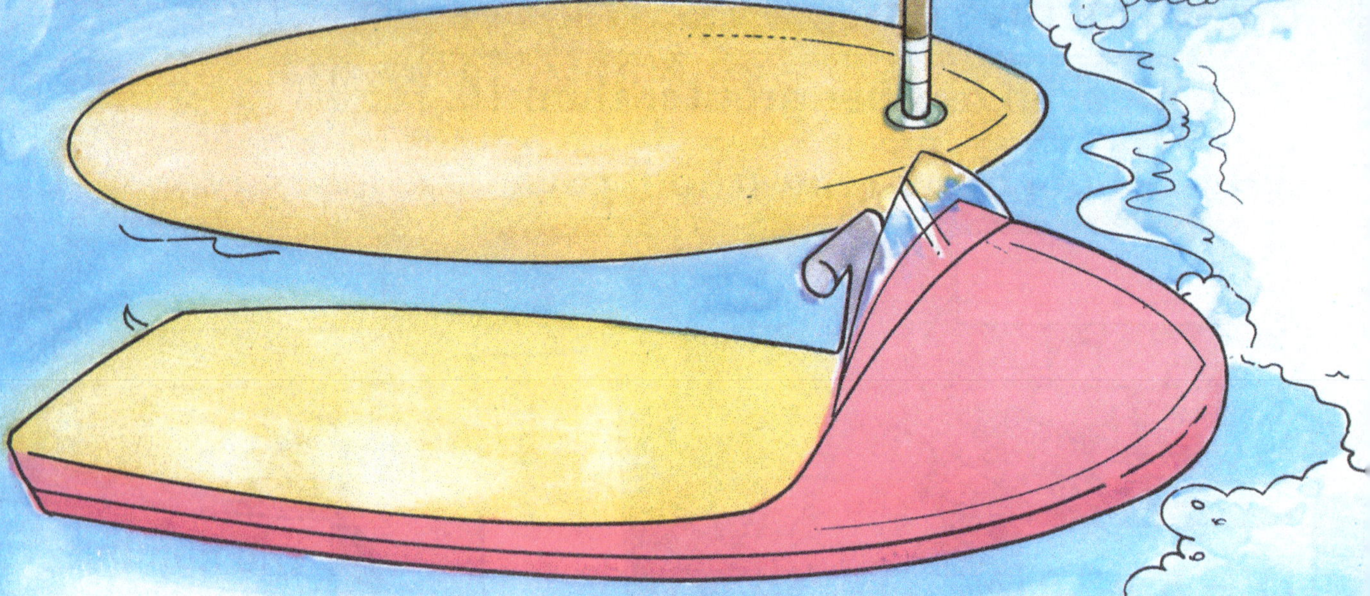

  6
+7
___

___

+
___

___

Find other stories for 13.

+	+	+	+	+	+
13	13	13	13	13	13

$2 + 3 + 8 = 13$

Find more stories like this for 13.

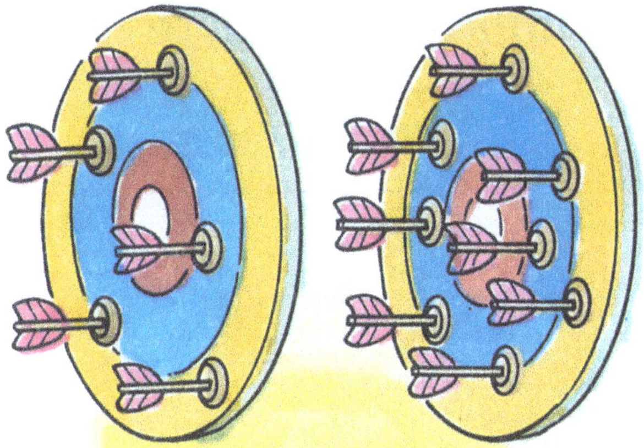

6 + 7 = 13

7 + 6 =

13 – 6 =

13 – 7 =

5 + 8 =

8 + 5 =

13 – 5 =

13 – 8 =

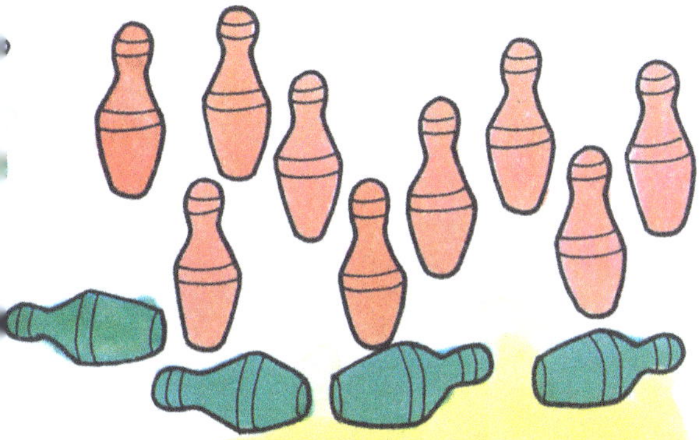

9 + 4 =

4 + 9 =

13 – 9 =

13 – 4 =

10 + 3 =

3 + 10 =

13 – 10 =

13 – 3 =

R24

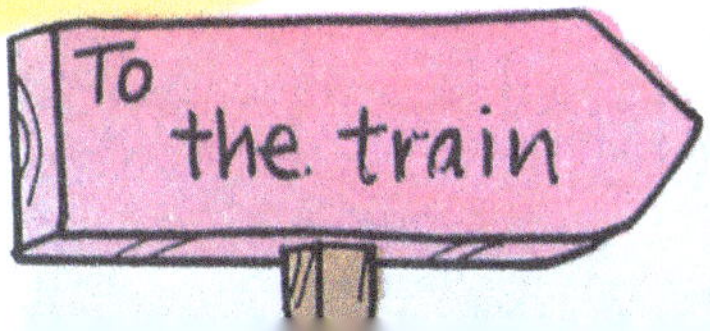

Train ride

Colour a carriage to match each answer.

Spooky Castle

Write the missing number.

This key opens the door.

Cross out flies to make 13.

13 children go in.
8 come out.

How many are still in? ____

Add to find the one that is different. 

The trapdoor key is in it.

Escape

Write the answers.

7 + 6 =

4 + 8 =

12 – 3 =

13 – 4 =

11 – 9 =

7 + 4 =

11 – 4 =

12 – 6 =

13 – 6 =

Colour the boxes

blue if the answer is odd,

red if the answer is even.

5	12	9	8	7	13
+8	–9	+4	+5	+5	–8

Which door has an even answer? Colour it red.

Problem solving

Colour three numbers which add to 12.

Amy had 13p.
She lost 7p in the sea.

How much is left? ___ p

Colour the monster that has two more black spots than green spots.

Find chests with the same answer.
Colour them to match.

The treasure is in the white chest.
Mark it ✗.

Stickers

Problem solving / Extension

Find the cost of a fox and a bear. ____

Find the cost of a fox, a tiger and a dog. ____

I spend 13p.
I buy 2 animals.
What do I buy? ____________

I have 8p.
I want a panda.
How much more do I need? ____

I have 12p. I buy a bear.
What else can I now buy?

fox or ________ or ________

Prizes

8. [+] [7] [=] [ ]

15. [−] [6] [=] [ ]

Now do these.

$7 + 9 =$ ☐ $6 + 8 =$ ☐ $10 + 9 =$ ☐

$16 - 7 =$ ☐ $14 - 8 =$ ☐ $17 - 9 =$ ☐

Who wins a prize? (✓)

[4] [+] [8] [+] [3] [+] [4] [=] ____

[9] [+] [2] [+] [5] [+] [2] [=] ____

[8] [+] [6] [+] [7] [−] [2] [=] ____

Halves

You need

Fold each in half.

Colour one half of each shape.

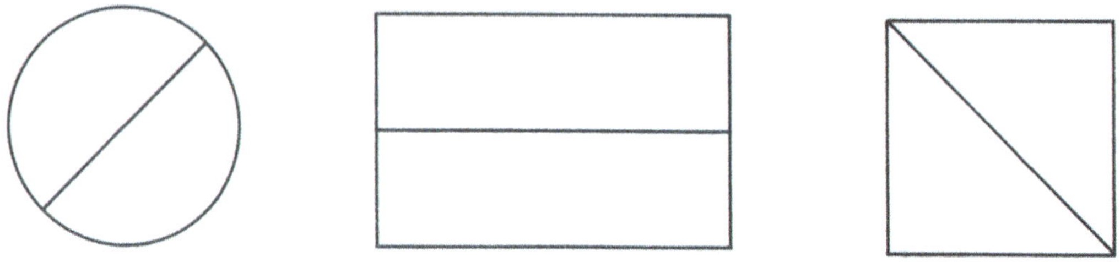

Tick the shapes that show halves.

Making halves

Cut out the four-strip.

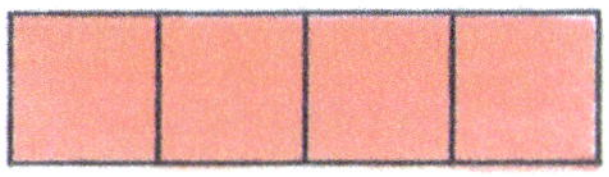

Fold it in half.

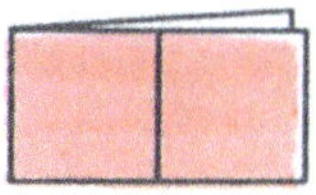

One half of 4 is ___ .

Cut out the six-strip.

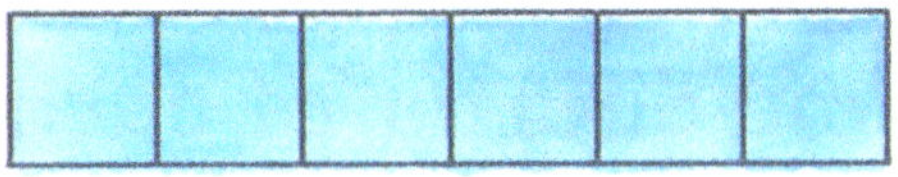

Fold it in half.

One half of 6 is ___ .

Make a tower with 8 cubes.

Halve it like this →

One half of 8 is ___ .

Use 10 cubes.

One half of 10 is ___ .

Use cubes. One half of 12 is ___ .

One half of 16 is ___ .

One half of 20 is ___ .

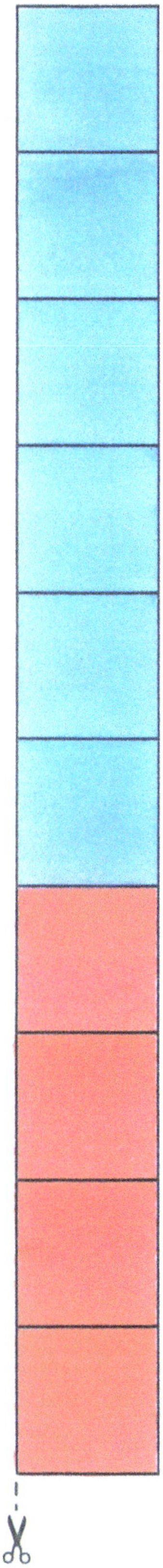

Quarters

You need

Fold each in quarters.

Colour one quarter of each shape.

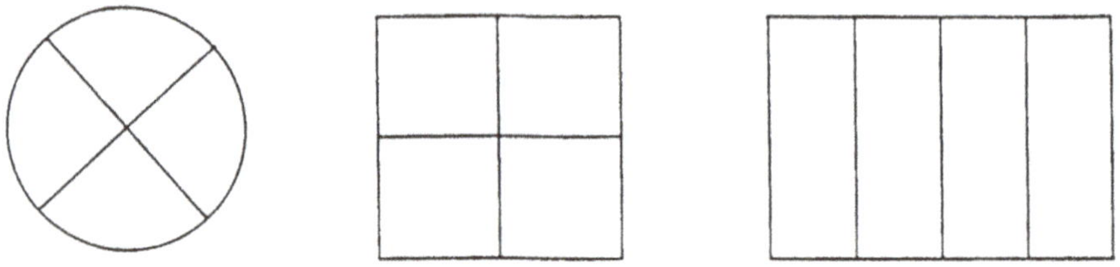

Tick the shapes that show quarters.

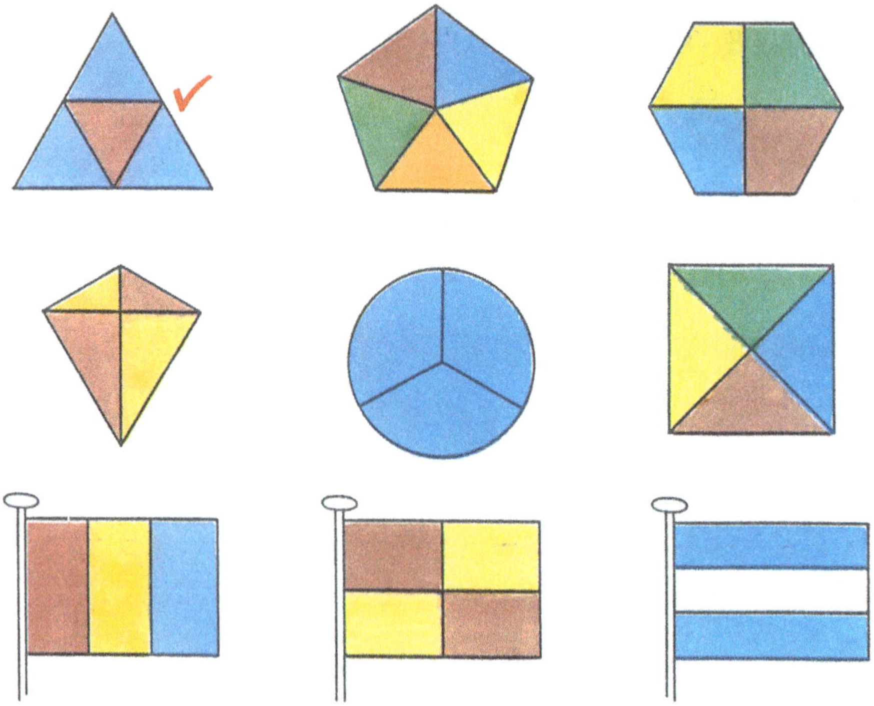

1	2	3	4	5	6	7	8	9	10	11	12	13	14	15	16	17	18	19	20	21	22	23

Heinemann is an imprint of Pearson Education Limited, a company incorporated in England and Wales, having its registered office at Edinburgh Gate, Harlow, Essex, CM20 2JE. Registered company number: 872828
ISBN 978 0 435 03094 0
First published 1991. Revised edition 1995. 19 28
Typeset and Illustrated by Oxprint Design. Printed and bound in Great Britain

ISBN 978-0-435030-94-0

SPMG

HEINEMANN MATHEMATICS 2

Name

WORKBOOK 4

Addition and Subtraction to 13, Halves and Quarters

Revised

Islands

Use cubes to add.

8 + 6 ☐

8 + 9 ☐

10 + 9 ☐

7 + 5 ☐

6 + 9 ☐

8 + 3 ☐

9 + 7 ☐

10 + 10 ☐

9 + 9 ☐

4 + 9 ☐

Use pennies. **How much is it to go to**

Mango Island and Nim-Nam-Noo ☐ p

Nim-Nam-Noo and Bear Island ☐ p ?

Use cubes to subtract. Match each boat to an island.

Write a subtraction story on this boat.

Extension

Amy and Jack go to Mango Island.
How much has each left?

Amy ___ p

Jack ___ p

To land on the island, find numbers which add to 11.

Use counters.

10 + 1				

How many ? ___
3 fly away.

11 − 3 = ___

How many ? ___
5 are picked.

11 − 5 = ___

How many ? ___
7 fall off.

11 − 7 = ___

How many ? ___
9 hide.

11 − 9 = ___

Bushes

Each bush has 11 flowers. Write stories.

9 + 2 = 11

2 + 9 = 11

11 – 2 = 9

11 – 9 = 2

8 + 3 =

3 + 8 =

11 – 3 =

11 – 8 =

7 + 4 =

4 + 7 =

11 – 4 =

11 – 7 =

6 + 5 =

5 + 6 =

11 – 5 =

11 – 6 =

Investigation

Find sets of 3 numbers which add to 11.

In the jungle

$$\begin{array}{r} 4 \\ +7 \\ \hline \end{array}$$ ___

$$\begin{array}{r} 11 \\ -3 \\ \hline \end{array}$$ ___

$$\begin{array}{r} 3 \\ +8 \\ \hline \end{array}$$ ___

$$\begin{array}{r} 11 \\ -9 \\ \hline \end{array}$$ ___

$$\begin{array}{r} 11 \\ -6 \\ \hline \end{array}$$ ___

11 − 4 = ___

11 − 8 = ___

5 + 6 = ___

11 − 2 = ___

11 − 1 = ___

The nest has 11 eggs.
4 fall out.

How many left? ___

11 flies
5 ants
How many more flies? ___

3 + 4 + 4 = ___

5 + 2 + 3 = ___

Buying food

How much does each spend?

Each child has 11p. They buy these things.
How much has each left?

Problem solving

Spend 11p.
What 3 things will you buy?

Nim-Nam-Noo

Put 12 Nim-nams on the island like this.

7 + 5 = 12

Find other ways to put 12 Nim-nams on the island.

☐ + ☐ = 12 ☐ + ☐ = 12

☐ + ☐ = 12 ☐ + ☐ = 12

☐ + ☐ = 12 ☐ + ☐ = 12

☐ + ☐ = 12 ☐ + ☐ = 12

Put 12 Nim-nams on the island like this.

5 + 4 + 3 = 12

Find other ways.

☐ + ☐ + ☐ = 12

☐ + ☐ + ☐ = 12

☐ + ☐ + ☐ = 12

Put 12 Nim-nams on the island.

If Noo eats 5, how many are left?

12 − 5 = ☐

12 − 9 = ☐   12 − 4 = ☐   12 − 10 = ☐

12 − 7 = ☐   12 − 6 = ☐   12 − 3 = ☐

Nim-nams

7 + 5 =

12 – 5 =

12 – 7 =

5 + 7 =

9 + 3 =

3 + 9 =

12 – 3 =

12 – 9 =

6 + 6 =

12 – 6 =

8 + 4 =

4 + 8 =

12 – 4 =

12 – 8 =

Nim-nam house

Find the answers. Colour them.

red	7 + 3	12 – 10	12 – 7
blue	12 – 4	8 + 3	6 + 6
green	6 + 3	12 – 9	12 – 8

How many altogether?

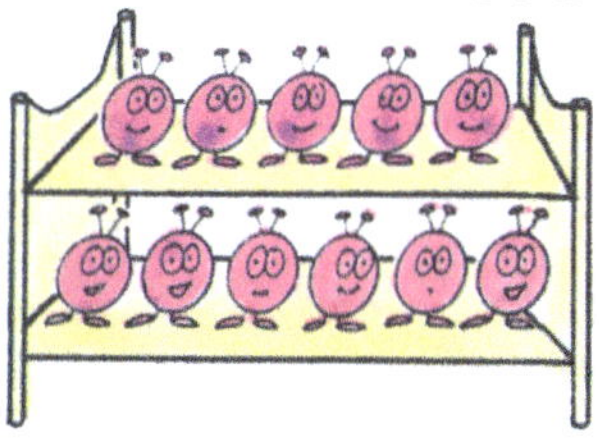

$$\begin{array}{r} 5 \\ +6 \\ \hline \end{array} \qquad \begin{array}{r} 8 \\ +4 \\ \hline \end{array} \qquad \begin{array}{r} 7 \\ +5 \\ \hline \end{array} \qquad \begin{array}{r} 3 \\ +9 \\ \hline \end{array}$$

$$\begin{array}{r} 5 \\ +7 \\ \hline \end{array} \qquad \begin{array}{r} 6 \\ +6 \\ \hline \end{array} \qquad \begin{array}{r} 3 \\ 4 \\ +5 \\ \hline \end{array} \qquad \begin{array}{r} 6 \\ 4 \\ +2 \\ \hline \end{array} \qquad \begin{array}{r} 4 \\ 4 \\ +3 \\ \hline \end{array}$$

Bear Island

In each cave,
colour three bears that add to make 12.

The school cave has

an even answer greater than 10.

Write School above the school cave.

Use these numbers to make the sums.

9 8 4 3

$$\begin{array}{r} 8 \\ +\ 4 \\ \hline 12 \end{array} \quad \begin{array}{r} \\ +\ \_ \\ \hline 11 \end{array} \quad \begin{array}{r} \\ +\ \_ \\ \hline 12 \end{array} \quad \begin{array}{r} \\ +\ \_ \\ \hline 13 \end{array}$$

$$\begin{array}{r} \\ -\ \_ \\ \hline 4 \end{array} \quad \begin{array}{r} \\ -\ \_ \\ \hline 6 \end{array} \quad \begin{array}{r} \\ -\ \_ \\ \hline 1 \end{array} \quad \begin{array}{r} \\ -\ \_ \\ \hline 5 \end{array}$$

Fun Island

Use 13 counters.

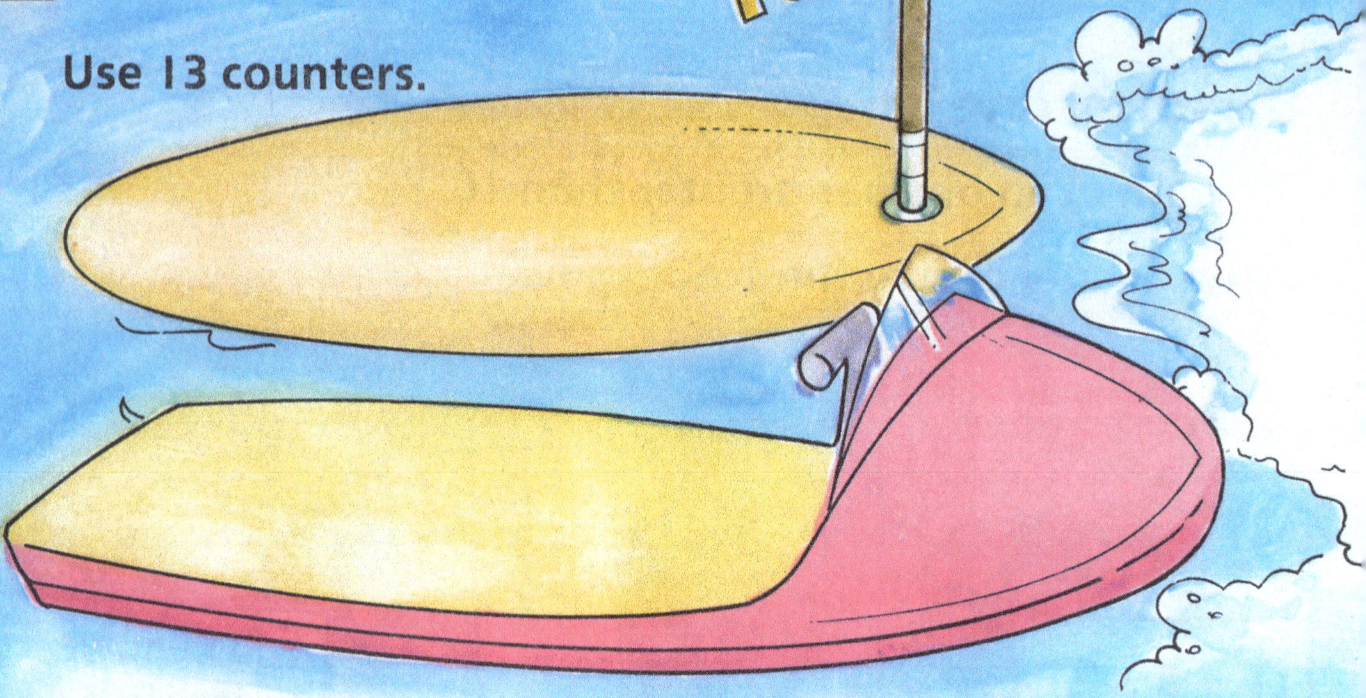

$$\begin{array}{r} 6 \\ +7 \\ \hline \\ \hline \end{array}$$

$$\begin{array}{r} \\ + \\ \hline \\ \hline \end{array}$$

Find other stories for 13.

+	+	+	+	+	+
13	13	13	13	13	13

2 + 3 + 8 = 13

Find more stories like this for 13.

$6 + 7 = 13$

$7 + 6 =$

$13 - 6 =$

$13 - 7 =$

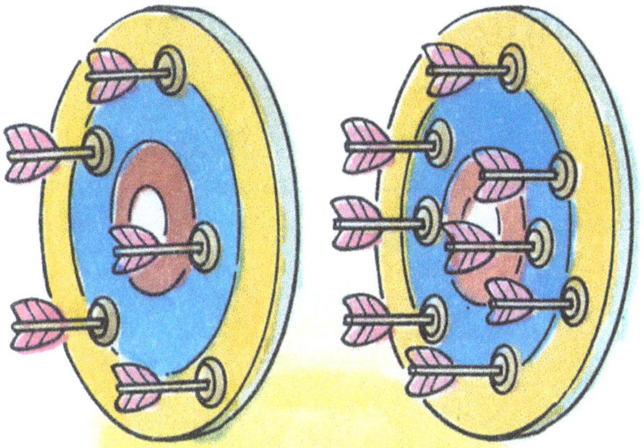

$5 + 8 =$

$8 + 5 =$

$13 - 5 =$

$13 - 8 =$

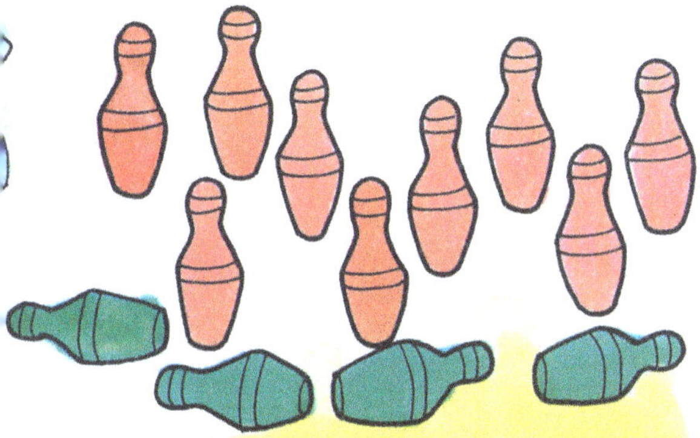

$9 + 4 =$

$4 + 9 =$

$13 - 9 =$

$13 - 4 =$

$10 + 3 =$

$3 + 10 =$

$13 - 10 =$

$13 - 3 =$

R24

Train ride

Colour a carriage to match each answer.

Spooky Castle

Write the missing number.

This key opens the door.

Cross out flies to make 13.

13 children go in.
8 come out.

How many are still in? ____

Add to find the one that is different.

The trapdoor key is in it.

Escape

Write the answers.

7 + 6 =	4 + 8 =	12 – 3 =
13 – 4 =	11 – 9 =	7 + 4 =
11 – 4 =	12 – 6 =	13 – 6 =

Colour the boxes

blue if the answer is odd,

red if the answer is even.

5 +8	12 –9	9 +4	8 +5	7 +5	13 –8

Which door has an even answer? Colour it red.

Problem solving

Colour three numbers which add to 12.

Amy had 13p.
She lost 7p in the sea.

How much is left? ___ p

Colour the monster that has two more black spots than green spots.

Find chests with the same answer.
Colour them to match.

The treasure is in the white chest.
Mark it ✗.

Stickers

Problem solving / Extension

Find the cost of a fox and a bear. ____

Find the cost of a fox, a tiger and a dog. ____

I spend 13p.
I buy 2 animals.
What do I buy? ____________

I have 8p.
I want a panda.
How much more do I need? ____

I have 12p. I buy a bear.
What else can I now buy?

fox or ________ or ________

Prizes

8. [+] [7] [=] ______

15. [−] [6] [=] ______

Now do these.

$7 + 9 =$ ☐ $6 + 8 =$ ☐ $10 + 9 =$ ☐

$16 - 7 =$ ☐ $14 - 8 =$ ☐ $17 - 9 =$ ☐

Who wins a prize? (✓)

[4] [+] [8] [+] [3] [+] [4] [=] ______

[9] [+] [2] [+] [5] [+] [2] [=] ______

[8] [+] [6] [+] [7] [−] [2] [=] ______

Halves

You need

Fold each in half.

Colour one half of each shape.

Tick the shapes that show halves.

Making halves

Cut out the four-strip.

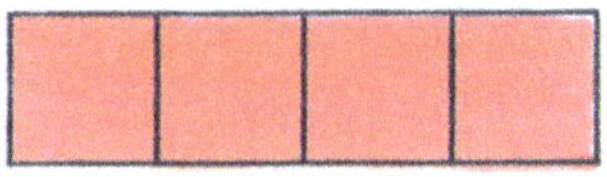

Fold it in half.

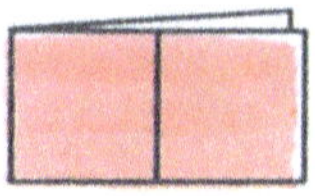

One half of 4 is ____ .

Cut out the six-strip.

Fold it in half.

One half of 6 is ____ .

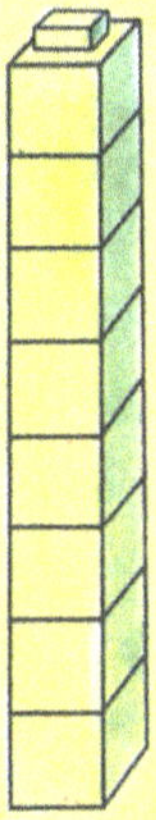

Make a tower with 8 cubes.

Halve it like this →

One half of 8 is ____ .

Use 10 cubes.

One half of 10 is ____ .

Use cubes. One half of 12 is ____ .

One half of 16 is ____ .

One half of 20 is ____ .

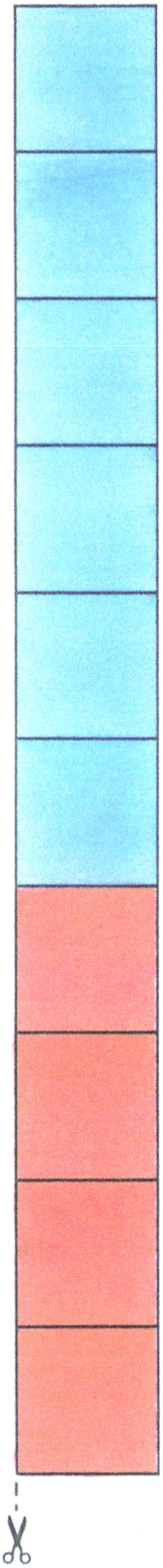

Quarters

You need

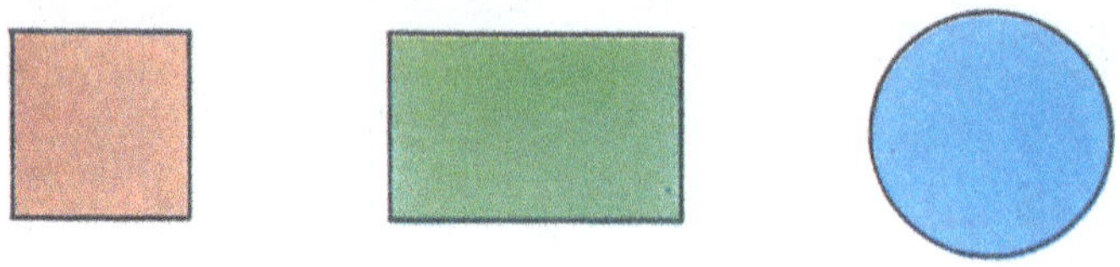

Fold each in quarters.

Colour one quarter of each shape.

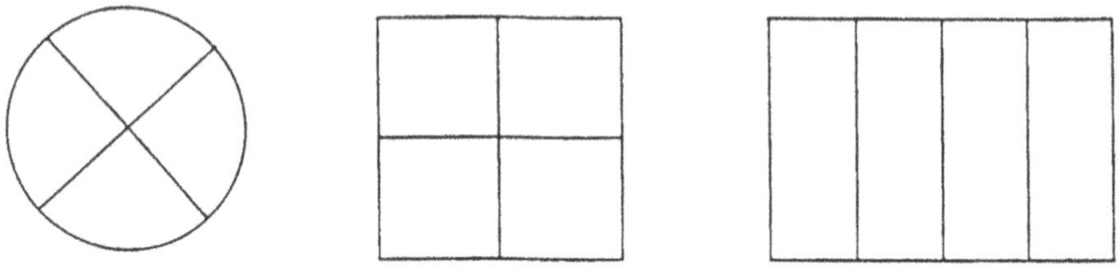

Tick the shapes that show quarters.

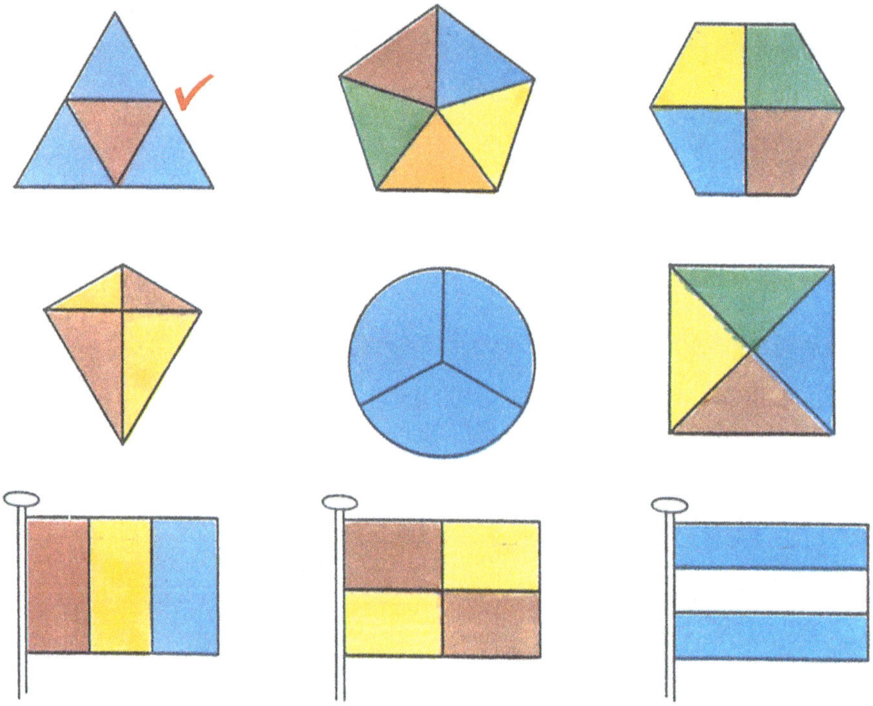

1	2	3	4	5	6	7	8	9	10	11	12	13	14	15	16	17	18	19	20	21	22	23

Heinemann is an imprint of Pearson Education Limited, a company incorporated in England and Wales, having its registered office at Edinburgh Gate, Harlow, Essex, CM20 2JE. Registered company number: 872828
ISBN 978 0 435 03094 0
First published 1991. Revised edition 1995. 19 28
Typeset and Illustrated by Oxprint Design. Printed and bound in Great Britain

ISBN 978-0-435030-94-0

HEINEMANN MATHEMATICS 2

Name

WORKBOOK 4

Addition and Subtraction to 13, Halves and Quarters

Revised

Islands

Use cubes to add.

8 + 6 = ☐

8 + 9 = ☐

10 + 9 = ☐

7 + 5 = ☐

6 + 9 = ☐

8 + 3 = ☐

9 + 7 = ☐

10 + 10 = ☐

9 + 9 = ☐

4 + 9 = ☐

Use pennies. How much is it to go to

Mango Island and Nim-Nam-Noo ☐ p

Nim-Nam-Noo and Bear Island ☐ p ?

Use cubes to subtract. Match each boat to an island.

Write a subtraction story on this boat.

Extension

Amy and Jack go to Mango Island.
How much has each left?

Amy ___ p

Jack ___ p

To land on the island, find numbers which add to 11.

Use counters.

10 + 1				

How many ? ___
3 fly away.

$11 - 3 =$ ___

How many ? ___
7 fall off.

$11 - 7 =$ ___

How many ? ___
5 are picked.

$11 - 5 =$ ___

How many ? ___
9 hide.

$11 - 9 =$ ___

Bushes

Each bush has 11 flowers. Write stories.

9 + 2 = 11

2 + 9 = 11

11 – 2 = 9

11 – 9 = 2

8 + 3 =

3 + 8 =

11 – 3 =

11 – 8 =

7 + 4 =

4 + 7 =

11 – 4 =

11 – 7 =

6 + 5 =

5 + 6 =

11 – 5 =

11 – 6 =

Investigation

Find sets of 3 numbers which add to 11.

In the jungle

$$\begin{array}{r} 4 \\ +7 \\ \hline \end{array}$$

$$\begin{array}{r} 11 \\ -3 \\ \hline \end{array}$$

$$\begin{array}{r} 3 \\ +8 \\ \hline \end{array}$$

$$\begin{array}{r} 11 \\ -9 \\ \hline \end{array}$$

$$\begin{array}{r} 11 \\ -6 \\ \hline \end{array}$$

11 − 8 = ___

11 − 4 = ___

5 + 6 = ___

11 − 2 = ___

11 − 1 = ___

The nest has 11 eggs.
4 fall out.

How many left? ___

11 flies
5 ants
How many more flies? ___

3 + 4 + 4 = ___

5 + 2 + 3 = ___

Buying food

How much does each spend?

Each child has 11p. They buy these things.
How much has each left?

Problem solving

Spend 11p.
What 3 things will you buy?

Nim-Nam-Noo

Put 12 Nim-nams on the island like this.

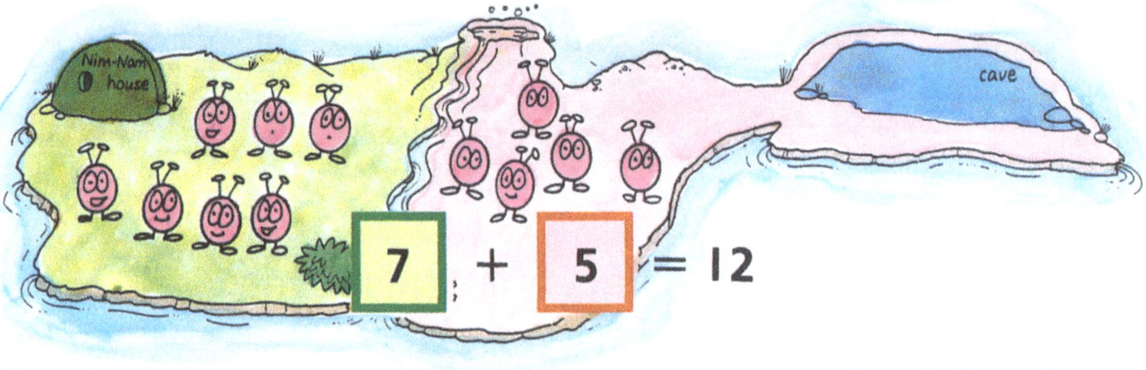

7 + 5 = 12

Find other ways to put 12 Nim-nams on the island.

☐ + ☐ = 12   ☐ + ☐ = 12

☐ + ☐ = 12   ☐ + ☐ = 12

☐ + ☐ = 12   ☐ + ☐ = 12

☐ + ☐ = 12   ☐ + ☐ = 12

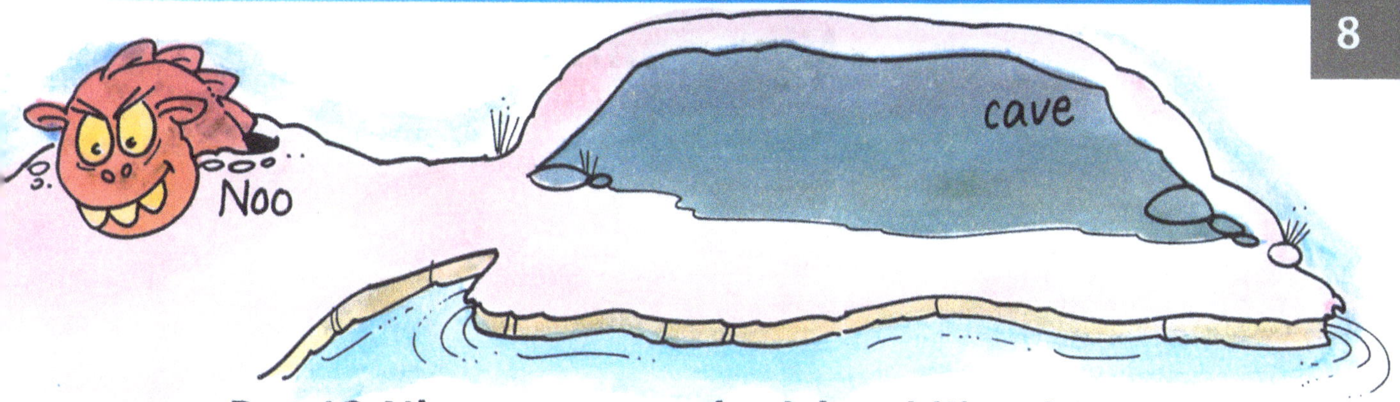

Put 12 Nim-nams on the island like this.

5 + 4 + 3 = 12

Find other ways.

☐ + ☐ + ☐ = 12

☐ + ☐ + ☐ = 12

☐ + ☐ + ☐ = 12

Put 12 Nim-nams on the island.

If Noo eats 5, how many are left?

12 − 5 = ☐

12 − 9 = ☐ 12 − 4 = ☐ 12 − 10 = ☐

12 − 7 = ☐ 12 − 6 = ☐ 12 − 3 = ☐

Nim-nams

$7 + 5 =$

$12 - 5 =$

$12 - 7 =$

$5 + 7 =$

$9 + 3 =$

$3 + 9 =$

$12 - 3 =$

$12 - 9 =$

$6 + 6 =$

$12 - 6 =$

$8 + 4 =$

$4 + 8 =$

$12 - 4 =$

$12 - 8 =$

Nim-nam house

Find the answers. Colour them.

red	7 + 3	12 – 10	12 – 7
blue	12 – 4	8 + 3	6 + 6
green	6 + 3	12 – 9	12 – 8

How many altogether?

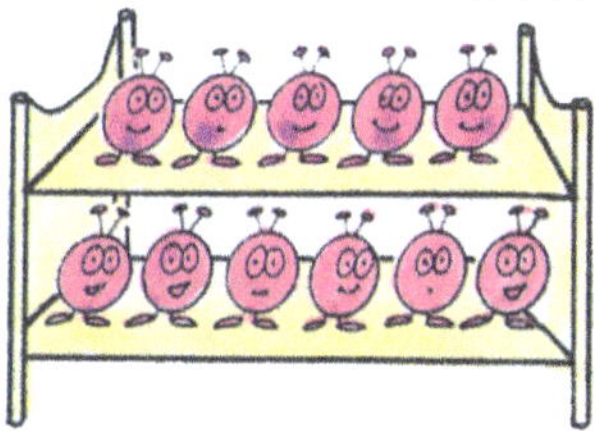

$$\begin{array}{r} 5 \\ +6 \\ \hline \\ \hline \end{array} \quad \begin{array}{r} 8 \\ +4 \\ \hline \\ \hline \end{array} \quad \begin{array}{r} 7 \\ +5 \\ \hline \\ \hline \end{array} \quad \begin{array}{r} 3 \\ +9 \\ \hline \\ \hline \end{array}$$

$$\begin{array}{r} 5 \\ +7 \\ \hline \\ \hline \end{array} \quad \begin{array}{r} 6 \\ +6 \\ \hline \\ \hline \end{array} \quad \begin{array}{r} 3 \\ 4 \\ +5 \\ \hline \\ \hline \end{array} \quad \begin{array}{r} 6 \\ 4 \\ +2 \\ \hline \\ \hline \end{array} \quad \begin{array}{r} 4 \\ 4 \\ +3 \\ \hline \\ \hline \end{array}$$

Bear Island

In each cave,
colour three bears that add to make 12.

The school cave has

an even answer greater than 10.

Write **School** above the school cave.

Use these numbers to make the sums.

9 8 4 3

8			
+ 4	+	+	+
12	11	12	13

−	−	−	−
4	6	1	5

Fun Island

Use 13 counters.

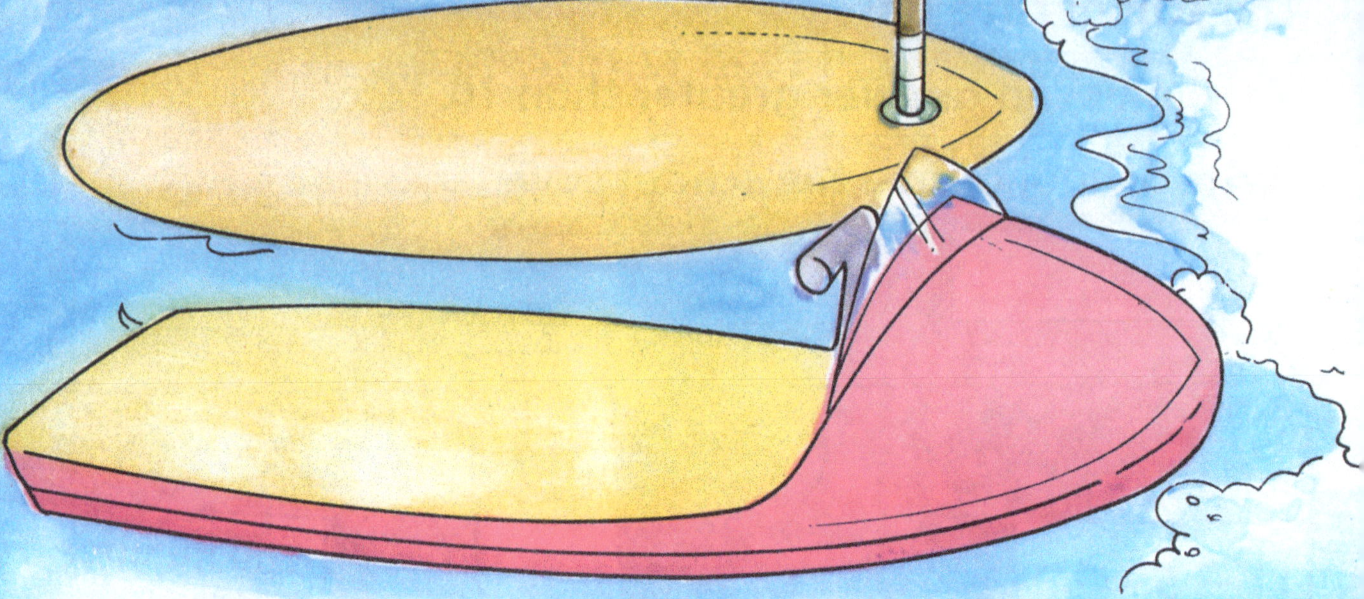

6
+7
___

___

+
___

___

Find other stories for 13.

+	+	+	+	+	+
13	13	13	13	13	13

$2 + 3 + 8 = 13$

Find more stories like this for 13.

6 + 7 = 13

7 + 6 =

13 − 6 =

13 − 7 =

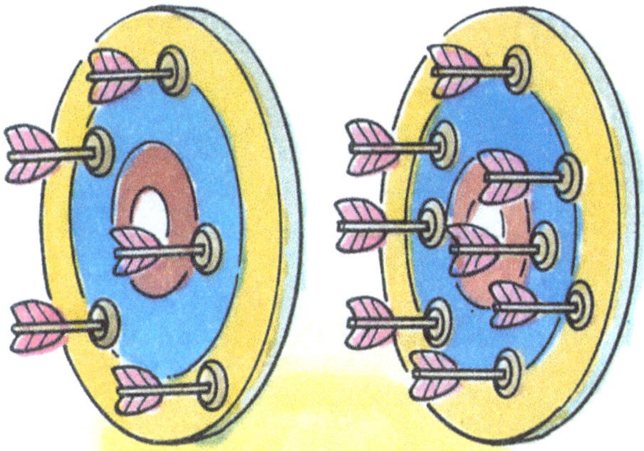

5 + 8 =

8 + 5 =

13 − 5 =

13 − 8 =

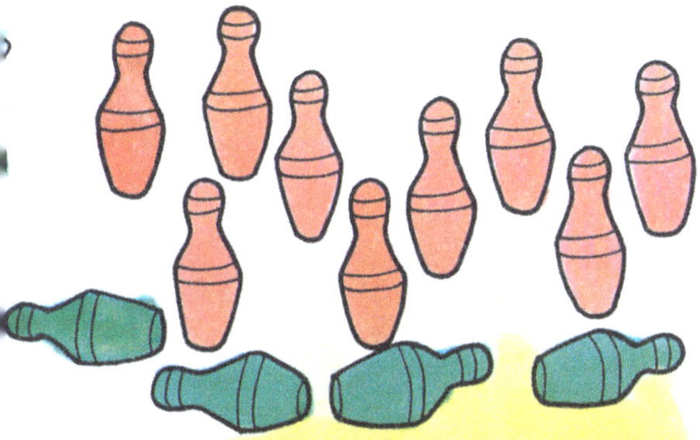

9 + 4 =

4 + 9 =

13 − 9 =

13 − 4 =

10 + 3 =

3 + 10 =

13 − 10 =

13 − 3 =

R 24

Train ride

Colour a carriage to match each answer.

Spooky Castle

Cross out flies to make 13.

Write the missing number.

This key opens the door.

13 children go in.
8 come out.

How many are still in? ___

Add to find the one that is different.

The trapdoor key is in it.

Escape

Write the answers.

7 + 6 =

4 + 8 =

12 – 3 =

13 – 4 =

11 – 9 =

7 + 4 =

11 – 4 =

12 – 6 =

13 – 6 =

Colour the boxes

blue if the answer is odd,

red if the answer is even.

5	12	9	8	7	13
+8	–9	+4	+5	+5	–8
___	___	___	___	___	___

Which door has an even answer? Colour it red.

Problem solving

Colour three numbers which add to 12.

Amy had 13p.
She lost 7p in the sea.

How much is left? ___ p

Colour the monster that has **two more** black spots than green spots.

Find chests with the same answer.
Colour them to match.

The treasure is in the white chest.
Mark it ✗ .

Stickers

Problem solving/Extension

Find the cost of a fox and a bear. ____

Find the cost of a fox, a tiger and a dog. ____

I spend 13p.
I buy 2 animals.
What do I buy? ____________

I have 8p.
I want a panda.
How much more do I need? ____

I have 12p. I buy a bear.
What else can I now buy?

fox or ________ or ________

Prizes

8. [+] [7] [=] ☐

15. [−] [6] [=] ☐

Now do these.

7 + 9 = ☐	6 + 8 = ☐	10 + 9 = ☐
16 − 7 = ☐	14 − 8 = ☐	17 − 9 = ☐

Who wins a prize? (✓)

[4] [+] [8] [+] [3] [+] [4] [=] ____

[9] [+] [2] [+] [5] [+] [2] [=] ____

[8] [+] [6] [+] [7] [−] [2] [=] ____

Halves

You need

Fold each in half.

Colour one half of each shape.

Tick the shapes that show halves.

Making halves

Cut out the four-strip.

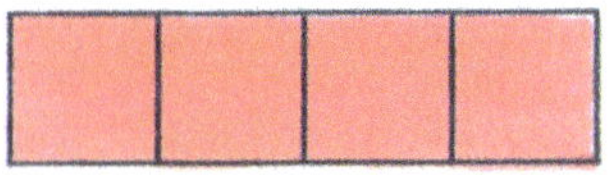

Fold it in half.

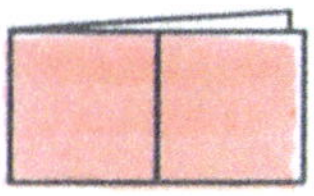

One half of 4 is ____ .

Cut out the six-strip.

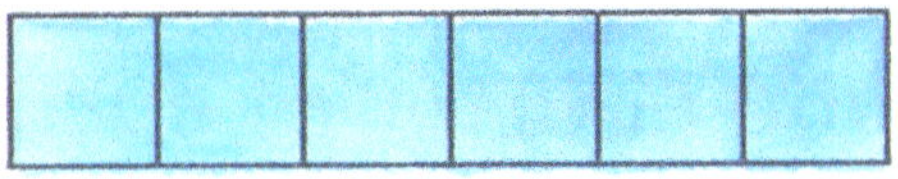

Fold it in half.

One half of 6 is ____ .

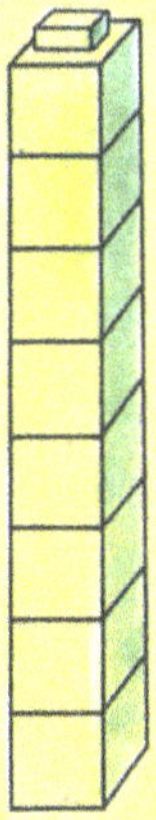

Make a tower with 8 cubes.

Halve it like this →

One half of 8 is ____ .

Use 10 cubes.

One half of 10 is ____ .

Use cubes. One half of 12 is ____ .

One half of 16 is ____ .

One half of 20 is ____ .

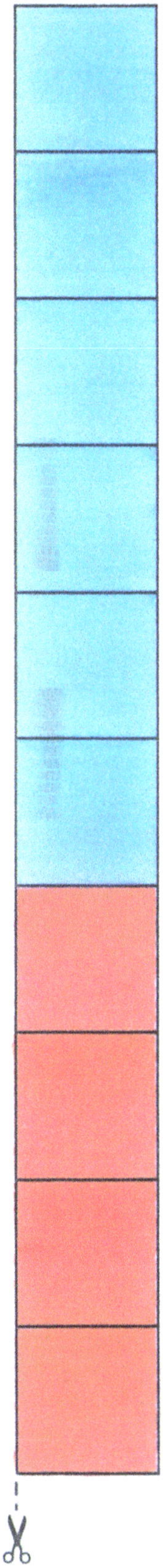

Quarters

You need

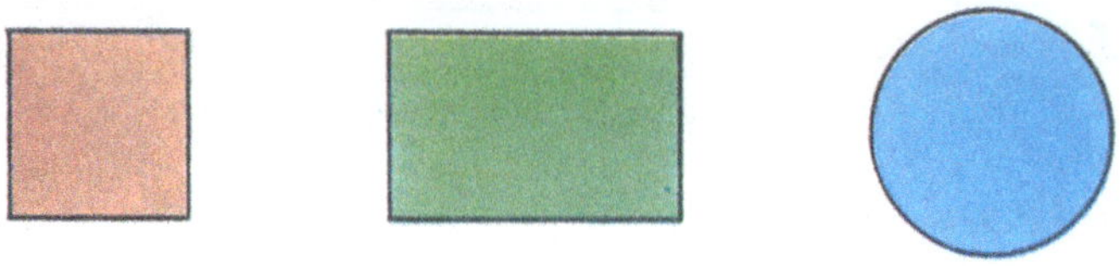

Fold each in quarters.

Colour one quarter of each shape.

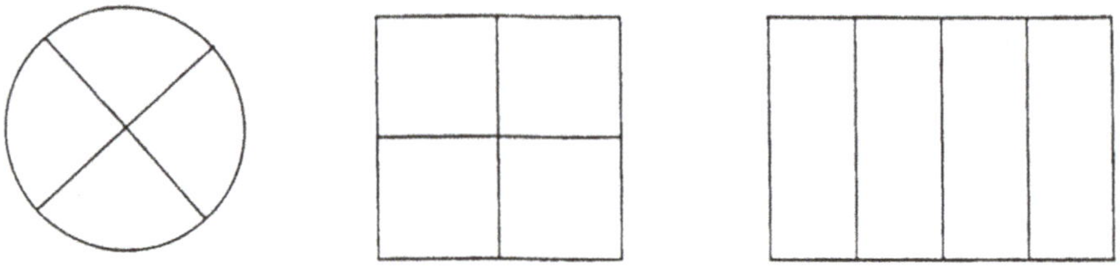

Tick the shapes that show quarters.

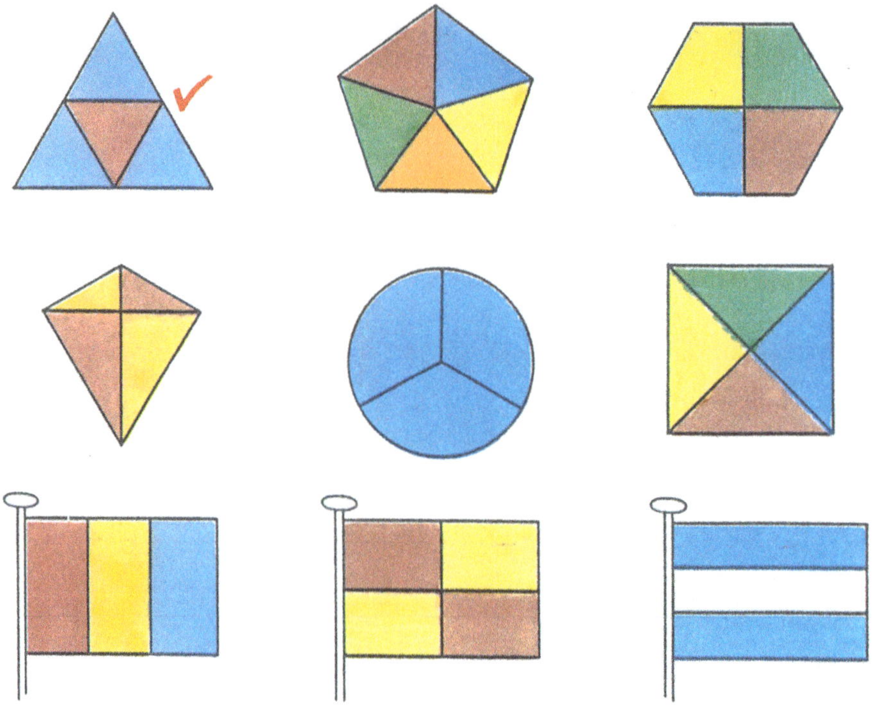

1	2	3	4	5	6	7	8	9	10	11	12	13	14	15	16	17	18	19	20	21	22	23

Heinemann is an imprint of Pearson Education Limited, a company incorporated in England and Wales, having its registered office at Edinburgh Gate, Harlow, Essex, CM20 2JE. Registered company number: 872828
ISBN 978 0 435 03094 0
First published 1991. Revised edition 1995. 19 28
Typeset and Illustrated by Oxprint Design. Printed and bound in Great Britain

ISBN 978-0-435030-94-0